THE CATHOLIC UNIVERSITY OF AMERICA
CANON LAW STUDIES
No. 181

CHAPTERS IN RELIGIOUS INSTITUTES

AN HISTORICAL SYNOPSIS AND COMMENTARY

BY THE

REV. GORDIAN LEWIS, C.P., J.C.L.
Priest of the Holy Cross Province

A DISSERTATION

Submitted to the Faculty of the School of Canon Law of the Catholic University of America in Partial Fulfillment of the Requirements for the Degree of Doctor of Canon Law

THE CATHOLIC UNIVERSITY OF AMERICA PRESS
WASHINGTON, D. C.
1943

Nihil Obstat:

HIERONYMUS D. HANNAN, A.M., LL.B., S.T.D., J.C.D.,
Censor Deputatus.

Washingtonii, die 24 maii, 1943.

Imprimi Potest:

HERMANNUS JOSEPHUS STIER, C.P., J.C.D.,
Praepositus Provincialis.

Chicagiae, die 24 maii, 1943.

Imprimatur:

✠ MICHAEL J. CURLEY, D.D.,
Archiepiscopus Baltimoriensis-Washingtoniensis.

Baltimorae, die 24 maii, 1943.

Printed by
THE PAULIST PRESS
New York, N. Y.
51

IN LOVING MEMORY

OF

MY MOTHER

TABLE OF CONTENTS

CHAPTER III

CHAPTER IV

INTRODUCTION

THE authority by which the internal life of a religious institute is governed is entrusted to the members of the institute itself and is exercised either individually or collegiately. The groups of persons exercising authority collegiately within these institutes are usually called chapters, but other designations are also used: such as, congregations, diets, etc. The present study is an attempt to trace the historical development of these collegiate superiors and to present a commentary on the canons determining their authority and governing their actions. It does not pretend to be an exhaustive treatment of the subject. A study of that kind would demand not only an analysis of the common law for religious but also a detailed investigation of the *ius religiosum comparatum*, that is, an analysis and comparison of the rules, constitutions, statutes, privileges, indults and legitimate customs of all religious institutes. The material for such a study was not available and, even if it were, the time within which this work had to be completed made such research impossible. This study, particularly in the canonical commentary, is, therefore, restricted to a consideration of the religious chapter as it is governed by the common law for religious; it will also attempt to note the matters in which the proper law may depart from this common legislation. The proper laws of particular institutes are cited sparingly and only by way of example.

If one considers the great number of these religious societies in the Church, each with its proper laws and privileges, the difficulty of writing a commentary common to all is quite evident. The writer decided that the most satisfactory way to do this was to limit his study to the aspects of a religious chapter in general; so, for the most part, no attempt is made to distinguish general, provincial and local chapters and to determine their constitution and competence. The types of chapter existing in any religious institute, and, consequently, their constitution and competence, depend entirely upon the constitutional law proper to that institute. The writer believes that what is said will apply to every general chapter and to any other chapter strictly so-called. When, however, provincial and local chapters are hardly more than a superior's council, much that is said will not apply to them. Particular applications will have to be made in the light of the proper constitutional law determining the nature of the chapter in question.

The writer takes this occasion to express his gratitude to his Congregation, especially to the Very Rev. Boniface Fielding, C.P., and the Very Rev. Herman Joseph Stier, C.P., J.C.D., provincials of the Holy Cross Province, for the opportunity given him to pursue advanced studies in Canon Law, to the Faculty of the School of Canon Law of the Catholic University of America, and to all who in any way aided in the preparation of this dissertation.

CHAPTER I

PRELIMINARY NOTIONS

A. *Definition of the Chapter*

(a) *Nominal Definition.* The English word "chapter" is derived from the Latin *capitulum* through the French *chapitre.*[1] The Latin form is a diminutive of *caput* and literally it means a "little head." By way of analogy it was used to designate a part or secof a book inasmuch as it was considered to contain one of the heads of doctrine. The use of the word to designate an assembly of religious can be traced back to the monastic practice of assembling daily to hear read a chapter of the Rule.[2] Gradually the place where this assembly took place came to be known as the chapterhouse and the meeting which was held there was called the chapter.[3] It was at these meetings that the superior proposed important matters in which he needed the counsel or consent of the brethren,[4] and to this practice is due the legal character which the religious chapter now

[1] The original French spelling was *chapitle* and the same form was used in English. Cf. *A New English Dictionary on Historical Principles,* edited by James A. H. Murray (Oxford: Clarendon Press, 1888—), v. "chapter."

[2] Calmét, *Commentaire Littéral, Historique et Moral sur la Régle de Saint Benôit* (2 vols. in 1, Paris, 1734), p. 163 (hereafter cited as Calmét, *Commentaire*); Bouix, *Tractatus de Capitulo* (3. ed., Parisiis, 1882), pars I, sec. I, cap. III, § 1 (hereafter cited as Bouix, *Tractatus de Capitulo*).

[3] Feasey, *Monasticism, What Is It?* (London, 1898), p. 230. For other explanations of the origin of the word cf. Calmét and Bouix, *loc. cit.* A rather quaint explanation, in conformity with the penchant of the writers in the early middle ages for inventing fantastic etymologies, is found in an eleventh century Customary: "Et potest convenienter dici capitulum, quasi capud licium, quoniam in eo terminantur lites, et si quae fuerint inter fratres discordiae aut dissensiones."—*Customary of the Benedictine Monasteries of St. Augustine, Canterbury, and St. Peter, Westminster* (2 vols., Vol. II edited by Sir Edward Maunde Thompson, London, 1904), p. 183.

[4] Knowles, *The Monastic Order in England* (Cambridge: University Press, 1940), p. 412.

possesses. In an historical development of this kind it is very difficult to say when the term "chapter" began to be used to designate this assembly. It was probably not before the Eighth Century; it can certainly be safely asserted that the usage was quite common in the Ninth Century.[5]

(b) *Real Definition.* Authors, generally, define a religious chapter in this way: An assembly of religious lawfully convened to treat of the interests of their institute or of some part of it.[6] This definition, however, is too generic and Larraona[7] rightly considers it as defining a religious chapter in a broad sense only, since, when a religious chapter is defined in this way, a religious council[8] could be called a chapter. How, then, is a religious chapter, strictly so-called, to be defined? The definition of a religious chapter should be such that it will apply to every chapter and only to a chapter. It should

[5] Perhaps the earliest use of it in extant literature is to be found in the Commentary on the Rule of St. Benedict written by Paul the Deacon (Paul Warnefrid) about the year 770. Cf. *Commentarium Pauli Warnefridi Diaconi Casinensis in Regulam S. P. N. Benedicti—Bibliotheca Casinensis* (5 vols., Casinensi, 1873), Vol. IV, *Florilegium,* p. 43 (hereafter this work will be referred to as Paul the Deacon, and the page references will be to this edition. in the *Bibliotheca Casinensis*).

[6] E. g., Fanfani, *De Iure Religiosorum ad Normam Codicis Iuris Canonici* (2. ed., Taurini-Romae: Marietti, 1925), n. 62 (hereafter cited as Fanfani, *De Iure Religiosorum*); Vermeersch, *De Religiosis Institutis et Personis Tractatus Canonico-moralis* (2. ed., 2 vols., Brugis, 1902-1904), I, n. 403 (hereafter cited as Vermeersch, *De Religiosis*); Wernz-Vidal, *Ius Canonicum ad Codicis Normam Exactum* (7 toms. in 8 vols., Romae: apud Aedes Universitatis Gregorianae, 1922-1938), III (1933), n. 103 (hereafter cited as Wernz-Vidal, *Ius Canonicum*); Coronata, *Institutiones Iuris Canonici ad Usum Utriusque Cleri et Scholarum* (5 vols., Taurini: Marietti, Vol. I, 2. ed., 1939), I, n. 535 (hereafter cited as Coronata, *Institutiones*); Schaefer, *De Religiosis ad Normam Codicis Iuris Canonici* (3. ed., Romae: S. A. L. E. R., 1940), p. 231 (hereafter cited as Schaefer, *De Religiosis*); Creusen-Garesché-Ellis, *Religious Men and Women in the Code* (3. English ed., Milwaukee: Bruce, 1940), n. 55 (hereafter cited as Creusen, *Religious Men and Women in the Code*).

[7] Larraona, "Commentarium Codicis" — *Commentarium pro Religiosis* (From 1935: *Commentarium pro Religiosis et Missionariis*) (Romae, 1920—) VI (1925), 428 (hereafter cited as *CpR* or *CpRM*).

[8] A religious council is the meeting of a superior, general, provincial or local, with the councillors prescribed by canon 516, § 1.

be such that it tells clearly what a religious chapter is and distinguishes it from any other canonical institute like it. With this end in view, from the distinguishing marks noted by authors, a religious chapter, strictly so-called, may be defined as: A collegiate moral person composed of those members of the religious institute who, according to the prescriptions of the constitutions and common law, possess the right of active suffrage, and constituted as an independent subject of authority in the internal government of the institute.

The first element in the definition is its existence as a collegiate moral person. When a religious chapter is so defined, its juridic nature is clearly established and it is, as it were, placed in its proximate juridic genus. There can be no doubt that the religious chapter is really a collegiate moral person for it possesses all the qualifications demanded for such juridic personality: viz. (1) a plurality of physical persons,[9] which, (2) for a religious or charitable end,[10] has been (3) perpetually[11] (4) established by competent ecclesiastical authority[12] as a subject capable of possessing juridic rights and du-

[9] I. e., at least three as demanded by canon 100, § 2: "Persona moralis collegialis constitui non potest, nisi ex tribus saltem personis physicis." This is required only when the moral person is originally constituted, later if only one member remains all the rights of the moral person devolve upon him. Cf. canon 102, § 2.

[10] Canon 100, § 1.

[11] Canon 102, § 1. That is, for an indefinite time. It is not required that the moral personality should always and continuously exercise its activity, but it is sufficient that it be established for an indefinite time even though its activity be exercised only at stated intervals. Cf. Wernz-Vidal, *Ius Canonicum*, II (2. ed., 1928), n. 34.

[12] Canon 100, § 1. In order to be established as a moral person recognition in law as a subject capable of possessing juridic rights and duties is sufficient. Cf. Chelodi, *Ius de Personis iuxta Codicem Iuris Canonici Praemisso Tractatu de Principiis et Fontibus I. C.* (2. ed. a Ernesto Bertagnolli, Tridenti: Libr. Edit. Tridentinum, 1927), n. 98 (hereafter cited as Chelodi, *Ius de Personis*); Cappello, *Summa Iuris Publici Ecclesiastici ad Normam Codicis Iuris Canonici et Recentiorum S. Sedis Documentorum Concinnata* (Romae: apud Aedes Universitatis Gregorianae, 1923), n. 49 (hereafter cited as Cappello, *Summa Iuris Publici*).

ties.[13] (1) It is clearly evident that a religious chapter is a collectivity or plurality of physical persons. (2) The purpose of a religious chapter, to have part in the internal government of a religious institute, is certainly a religious end. (3) Its perpetuity is coterminous with that of the religious institute, province, or house, recognized by the Code as moral persons,[14] which it represents. (4) It is established as a subject capable of juridic rights and duties by the Rules and Constitutions, the particular law of the institute, which determine and establish the internal hierarchy of government of the institute.[15] The chapter is an integral part of this hierarchy of government. Moreover, the chapter is recognized in the Code as capable of possessing juridic rights and duties; e. g., of possessing dominative or jurisdictional power [16] and rights of election,[17] with the corresponding duties of exercising these rights according to the prescriptions of law. All of this proves conclusively that the religious chapter is truly a collegiate moral person.

A further question here presents itself. Is the moral personality of the chapter a new and distinct personality or is it the same personality as that of the religious institute or part of it which as a chapter it represents? Larraona [18] and Coronata,[19] who seems to rely upon Larraona, say it is not a new moral personality but merely a representation of the moral personality of the religious institute

[13] The latter part of this qualification is not mentioned in the Code when treating of moral persons; it is, however, the essential note of juridic personality; thus Wernz-Vidal (*Ius Canonicum,* II, n. 1) say: "Persona heic non sumitur sensu philosophico sed iuridico; quo sensu persona est subjectum iurium et officiorum." Cf. also Cappello, *Summa Iuris Canonici in Usum Scholarum Concinnata* (3 vols., Romae: apud Aedes Universitatis Gregorianae, Vols. I-II, 3. ed., 1938-1939), I, nn. 183, 207 (hereafter cited as Cappello, *Summa Iuris Canonici*).

[14] E. g., canon 536, § 1: "Si persona moralis (sive religio, sive provincia, sive domus). . . ."

[15] "Ius peculiare cuiuslibet Religionis, scilicet illae leges, ipsius propriae, quibus vita interna, sive quoad regimen sive quoad membrorum officia iura, ordinatur vocantur in codice *Regulae et constitutiones.*"—Larraona, "Commentarium Codicis"—*CpR,* IV (1923), 112.

[16] Canon 501, § 1.

[17] Canons 506, 507.

[18] "Commentarium Codicis"—*CpR,* VI (1925), 429, note (138).

[19] *Institutiones,* I, n. 535.

or part of it, as the case may be. It is difficult to understand upon what foundation they base this statement. Neither author presents any reasons for his opinion. On the contrary, the religious chapter seems to be a really distinct moral person since: (1) the qualifications for incorporation into the chapter are distinct from the qualifications for incorporation into the moral person it represents; (2) the rights and duties which reside in the chapter as in a subject do not reside in the moral person it represents as in a subject; (3) the collectivities in which the moral personality resides are established by authorities specifically diverse.

(1) The qualifications for incorporation into the chapter are distinct from the qualifications for incorporation into the moral person it represents. It is true, indeed, that every member of the chapter is a member of the moral person represented by the chapter, but the converse is not true. For to be incorporated into a religious institute and, consequently, into a particular province and house of that institute, the only qualification required is the act of religious profession; [20] but in order to possess the right of active suffrage in chapter some further qualification is necessary; e. g., for the local chapter, perpetual or solemn profession, a determined number of years of profession, the reception of sacred orders, etc.; for the provincial or general chapter, election, nomination, or some other form of designation.[21]

(2) The rights and duties which reside in the chapter as in a subject do not reside in the moral person it represents as in a sub-

[20] This was established in principle in the Decretals of Gregory IX: ". . . cum habitus non faciat monachum, sed professio regularis."—C. 22, X, *de regularibus et transeuntibus ad religionem*, III, 31. Cf. Schaefer (*De Religiosis*, p. 580): "Professus per suam professionem (traditionem) Religioni ut verum membrum incorporatur."

[21] This must be understood as a general rule suffering exceptions. For in regard to the local chapter the rules and constitutions could grant any member of the community, even though only temporarily professed, the right of suffrage. Canon 578, 3°, it is true, denies to those temporarily professed the right of active suffrage, but it makes provision for contrary provisions of the constitutions. For provincial and general chapters some further qualification, besides religious profession, seems always required. This question of the right of suffrage will be dealt with in a later chapter.

ject. It is certainly true that all the juridic rights which a chapter possesses are exercised in behalf of the moral person it represents. It is, however, one thing to say that a person possesses certain rights as a subject and quite a different thing to say that certain rights are exercised in behalf of that person. In this latter case the person should be called the object of the rights rather than the subject. This seems to be the case in regard to the rights possessed by the chapter in relation to the moral person it represents.

(3) The collectivities in which the moral personality resides are established by authorities specifically diverse. That is, the one is always established by the act of a competent superior, the other is established by law. For a religious institute, a province or a house is always established by the act of a competent superior; [22] the chapter, on the contrary, is established by the Rules and Constitutions, the particular law of the institute, which determines and establishes the internal hierarchy of government in the institute, and the chapter, as has been said, is an integral part of this hierarchy of government. The arguments presented here, while not at all conclusive, do seem to point to the fact that the chapter is a new moral person distinct from the moral personality which it represents.

The second part of the definition, composed of those members of the religious institute who, according to the prescriptions of the constitutions and common law, possess the right of active suffrage, determine the composition of the chapter and, by demanding of the physical persons composing it the qualification of being members of a religious institute completely distinguishes it from all other moral personalities which are either merely clerical or merely lay in character; e. g., the chapter of canons.[23]

The third and final part of the definition, constituted as an independent subject of authority in the internal government of the institute, determines the purpose for which the chapter has been con-

[22] For the procedure in the establishing of a religious institute, cf. canon 492, §§ 1, 2; Schaefer, *De Religiosis,* pp. 122, 127-129; Coronata, *Institutiones,* I, nn. 510, 512, 516. Of a province, cf. canon 494, § 1; Schaefer, *De Religiosis,* pp. 149-150; Coronata, *Institutiones,* I, nn. 519-520. Of a religious house cf. canons 495-497; Schaefer, *op. cit.,* pp. 153 ss.; Coronata, *op. cit.,* nn. 522, 523.

[23] Cf. canon 391, § 1.

stituted as a moral person and by which it is distinguished from other collectivities exercising authority in the institute, that is, from religious councils. The expression, independent subject, must be properly understood. It is not intended to mean that the chapter is completely autonomous, but that the acts which are performed by the chapter are to be attributed to the moral personality of the chapter and not to any other superior. It is in just this respect that the religious chapter differs from the religious council; for the council is constituted to assist or restrict the superior in the exercise of his power, either by advice or by consent according to the norm of canon 105, but the acts performed are the acts of the superior.[24] The chapter, on the contrary, is not constituted to assist the superior, but has an authority of its own distinct from the authority of any superior,[25] even, according to Larraona, specifically different.[26] This authority is to be exercised collegiately according to the norm of canon 101 and the acts performed are to be attributed to the collegiate personality.[27]

In the definition which has been given of a religious chapter there are contained, moreover, the elements of the philosophic definition *per causas*. The *material* cause, that from which a thing is made, is found in the words: those members of the religious institute who, according to the prescriptions of the constitutions and common law, possess the right of active suffrage. The *formal* cause,

[24] Larraona, "Commentarium Codicis"—*CpR,* VI (1925), 429-430; Wernz-Vidal, *Ius Canonicum,* III, nn. 103, 110.

[25] Wernz-Vidal, *Ius Canonicum,* III, n. 103.

[26] ". . . Nec solum *gradu* differt haec potestas capitulorum et consiliorum, sed aliquo modo, generatim loquendo, etiam specie, quia potestas consiliorum ad legum applicationem, ad regimen ordinarium, ad negotia non adeo gravia vel quae differri non possunt solet restringi dum, ex adverso, potestas capitulorum ad omnia extenditur intra propriam ipsorum sphaeram. Ergo potestas capitulorum est *substantiva* in suo ordine, potestas superiorum et consiliorum relate ad potestatem capitulorum est *adiectiva* et *exequutiva.* Si ex iure constitutionali comparationem desumamus capitula in genere Cameris legislativis, superiores et consilia ministris aequiparari possunt."—"Commentarium Codicis"—*CpR,* VI (1925), 429 and note (137).

[27] Wernz-Vidal, *Ius Canonicum,* III, 103; Larraona, "Commentarium Codicis" —*CpR,* VI (1925), 430.

that by which a thing is placed in a definite category of being, and the *efficient* cause, that by which it is brought into being, are found in the words: collegiate moral person. It is this quality of moral personality that places this collectivity in a definite juridic genus and from the positive prescriptions of law only some competent ecclesiastical authority can be the efficient cause of such moral personality. The *final* cause, the purpose for which a thing exists, is found in the words: constituted as an independent subject of authority in the internal government of the institute.

From all that has been said it seems to be quite clear that the definition as given is sufficiently accurate so that it may be said to define a religious chapter strictly so-called.

B. *Species of the Chapter*

The chapters in religious institutes can be distinguished in various ways, depending upon the basis on which the division is founded.

1. The most well known division is based upon the moral personality which the chapter represents. Chapters distinguished upon this foundation are called:

(a) *General,* one which represents a whole religious institute.

(b) *Provincial,* representing a religious province.

(c) *Local* or *conventual,* representing a religious house.[28]

2. Considering the end for which the chapter is convoked religious chapters are divided into:

(a) *Chapters of affairs,* to decide on business of various kinds committed to the chapter.

(b) *Chapters of election,* to elect the various superiors of the institute.

(c) *Mixed chapters,* for conducting both types of business. Practically all general chapters are of this kind.

3. From the occasion or the time when chapters are convoked, they are called:

[28] This division applies particularly to the more centralized religious institutes, like the Mendicant Orders. All religious institutes do not have all these chapters. The provincial chapter is lacking in many diocesan congregations and the local chapter in many modern congregations. The kinds of chapters to be held in any religious institute are determined by its Constitutions.

(a) *Ordinary,* those prescribed by the constitutions.

(b) *Extraordinary,* called at a time or for a cause not provided for in the constitutions.[29]

The *chapter of faults* is an ascetic practice and has no juridic significance.

C. *Formal Parts of the Chapter*

The formal parts of a chapter are the *convocation,* the *celebration,* and the *confirmation.* Since the chapter is a collegiate moral person, its decisions must be made by suffrage. This is of the essense of collegiate action. This voting, moreover, should take place in an actual assembly and not separately and individually. Convocation is the ordinary means by which this assembly is brought together and is, therefore, ordinarily necessary. Finally, it is sometimes necessary, i. e., when it is prescribed by law as shall be seen, that the results of the collegiate action be submitted to a competent superior for confirmation.

[29] This is the meaning given to these terms by Larraona ("Commentarium Codicis"—*CpR,* VI [1925], 430-431). The *Normae* of 1901 (Art. 206-207, 210) considered as an ordinary chapter one celebrated after a certain definite period determined by the constitutions, e. g., every three, six, or twelve years; any other chapter was extraordinary.

Part I

Historical Synopsis

CHAPTER II

THE MONASTIC ERA

Article 1. Chapters in the Monastic Literature

Section I. In Egyptian and Oriental Monasticism

1. Before Pachomius

The early beginnings of the religious life in the Eastern Church are all eremitic in character and it is useless to seek here for any traces of a chapter, because their mode of life was all they had in common. It is true that on certain occasions they gathered for divine service, but of any closer bond than this there is no evidence. Even superiors and subjects in the strict sense are not found and the only thing resembling it is the relationship of master and disciple.[1]

2. In Pachomian Cenobitism

The first gatherings resembling chapters are to be found in cenobitism as established by St. Pachomius. Two annual gatherings were held by the Pachomian monks. The first was of a liturgical character when they gathered at Easter to celebrate in common the great feast of the Resurrection. The second was administrative;

[1] Butler, *Benedictine Monachism* (2. ed., London: Longmans, Green & Co., 1924), p. 12.

the monks all gathered at Pabau in the month of August and the superiors gave a report on the condition of their houses and superiors were appointed.[2] Beyond the fact that this meeting was held and a report of the matters treated, the sources yield nothing definite.[3]

Just how much influence Pachomius had on Western Monasticism it is very hard to say. It seems likely that St. Jerome's latin translation of the Rule of Pachomius was well known in the West and internal criticism shows some close resemblances between the Rule of Pachomius and the Rule of St. Benedict.[4] The degree of this influence would, however, be a matter of conjecture.

3. In Basilian Monachism

Basilian monachism was an advance as far as community life was concerned over that established by St. Pachomius, but in the Basilian Literature there are no clear references to any assembly like a chapter. The Rule of St. Basil is more in the nature of a catechetical instruction on the monastic life, and supposes the monastery as already established and functioning. The most that can be found concerning the existence of a chapter are vague references

[2] *Praefatio in Regulam S. Pachomii,* 6, 8—Migne, *Patrologiae Cursus Completus, Series Latina* (221 vols., Parisiis, 1844-1855), XXIII, 64 (hereafter cited as *MPL*); *Regula S. Pachomii,* c. 27—*MPL,* XXIII, 68; *Epistolae et Verba Mystica S. Pachomii,* VII—*MPL,* XXIII, 96.

[3] Butler (*The Lausaic History of Palladius—Texts and Studies,* VI [2 vols., Cambridge, 1898-1904], p. 235), writing of Pachomian monachism, says: "The most remarkable feature about it is that (like Citeaux in a later age) it almost at once assumed the shape of a fully organized congregation or order, with a superior general and a system of visitation and general chapters,—in short all the machinery of centralized government, such as does not appear in the monastic world until the Cistercian and Mendicant orders arose in the twelfth and thirteenth centuries." However, the only authority he gives to support this claim is his years of familiarity with the literature of this period (p. 228).

[4] Butler, *Sancti Benedicti Regula Monasteriorum, Editio Critico-Practica* (editio altera, Friburgi Brisgoviae: Herder, 1927), *passim* (hereafter all references to the Rule of St. Benedict will be made to this edition and will be cited as *Regula S. Benedicti*); *Benedictine Monachism,* p. 20; Chapman, *St. Benedict and the Sixth Century* (London: Sheed & Ward, 1929), p. 33.

to elections[5] and advice to the superior to take counsel.[6] There is no detailed direction however about the manner in which this was to be done. As a matter of fact, anything democratic is definitely contrary to St. Basil's idea. It was just in order to avoid anything like popular government in the absence of the superior, that he made provision that there should be a second in authority who should rule when the superior was not present.[7]

Section II. Western Monasticism

While it is possible that the assembly of the Pachomian monks might have been in the nature of a general chapter, so far as can be determined it exerted no influence outside of Egypt. In the West, however, toward the end of the Monastic Era, general and provincial chapters were permanently instituted. In order, therefore, to present the material in this section in an orderly fashion, the development of the local or conventual chapter will be traced first, and then that of the provincial and general chapter will be treated.

I. The Local or Conventual Chapter.

1. *Before the Rule of St. Benedict*

The monastic life was introduced into the Western Church from the East, particularly from Egypt, and it preserved for some time the characteristics of Egyptian monachism. While it tended to become more and more cenobitical, a survey of pre-Benedictine monasticism over the whole of the West shows that the founders felt that the closer their life approximated that of the Egyptian hermits the more nearly perfect it was.[8] Cassian, one of the founders of

[5] *Regulae Fusius Tractatae,* XLIII—Migne, *Patrologiae Cursus Completus, Series Graeca* (161 vols., Parisiis, 1857-1866), XXXI, 1030 (hereafter cited as *MPG*).

[6] *Regulae Brevius Tractatae,* CIV—*MPG,* XXXI, 1155.

[7] *Regulae Fusius Tractatae,* XLV—*MPG,* XXXI, 1031.

[8] Butler, *Benedictine Monachism,* pp. 17-22.

monasteries in the West, was certainly of this opinion.[9] In such an atmosphere an institute like the religious chapter would hardly be found.

2. *In the Rule of St. Benedict*

The rule of St. Benedict provides the first definite prescriptions for the conventual chapter. The expression itself is not used, but in the third chapter of his rule, St. Benedict gives the community a voice in the affairs of the monastery.[10] This chapter of the rule clearly establishes two things. The first is that there are two bodies of councillors: the whole community for important matters, and the seniors for matters of lesser importance. The other point is that the suffrage of the brethren is only consultative, for after the abbot has heard the advice of the brethren it is left to him to decide what is to be done.

The rule does not say what are the important or less important matters, who are to be classed as seniors, or who are to be considered as members of the community except that novices are not received into the community until after their probation is over.[11] All these points gradually became determined by custom and practice. When it is said that the rule does not indicate what are the important matters, one exception must be made. Chapter LXIV gives the whole community the right to choose the abbot.[12] It has been a matter of dispute from the earliest times whether this was a true election or not. It is a question which cannot be settled here. It is sufficient for

[9] *Joannis Cassiani Conlationes* XXIIII, edited by Michael Petsching—*Corpus Scriptorum Ecclesiasticorum Latinorum,* Vol. XIII, pars II (Vindobonae, 1886), Con. XVIII, IIII, p. 509 (hereafter cited as *CSEL*).

[10] "Quotiens aliqua praecipua agenda sunt in monasterio, convocet abbas omnem congregationem, et dicat unde agitur. Et audiens consilium fratrum tractet apud se, et quod utilius iudicaverit faciat. Ideo autem omnes ad concilium vocari diximus, quia saepe iuniori Dominus revelat quod melius est. . . . Si qua vero minora agenda sunt in monasterii utilitatibus, seniorum tantum utatur consilio. . . ." *Regula Sancti Benedicti,* c. III, pp. 19-20.

[11] *Regula S. Benedicti,* c. LVIII, pp. 105-110.

[12] "In abbatis ordinatione illa semper consideretur ratio, ut hic constituatur quem sive omnis concors congregatio secundum timorem Dei, sive etiam pars quamvis parva congregationis saniore consilio elegerit."—*Regula S. Benedicti,* c. LXIV, p. 117.

the purpose of this study to note that in St. Benedict's plan the community did have some voice in the choice of its abbot. An even more difficult question is the meaning of the expression in the rule: "*pars quamvis parva congregationis saniore consilio elegerit.*" All the commentators on the rule have tried to determine what St. Benedict meant. A good summing up of the various opinions can be found in the commentary of Dom Paul Delatte.[13]

3. *In the Other Rules of This Period*

There were many other rules written during this period but an examination of them shows no advance on the prescriptions of St. Benedict; no one contains even as much.[14] Two points, however, might be mentioned. The Rule of Chrodegang, in the recension of d'Achery, shows that the daily chapter was in use among the Canons Regular.[15] St. Caesarius of Arles in the rule which he wrote for nuns (c. 542) places the election of the abbess in the hands of the community.[16]

4. *In Other Monastic Literature*

Any attempt to take up each of the individual sources which come under this heading and give the developments to which it bears witness in the history of the monastic chapter would only result in confusion and needless repetition, so the whole period, beginning with the Commentary of Paul the Deacon (c. 770) and ending with the rise of the Mendicants (c. 1200), will be viewed as a whole. As a help to an orderly presentation the division of the section will have as its basis the various elements of the chapter.

[13] *The Rule of St. Benedict, A Commentary,* translated by Dom Justin McCann (London: Burns, Oates & Washbourne, 1921), pp. 444-445.

[14] Most of these rules can be found in a convenient form for consultation in the *Concordia Regularum Patrum* of St. Benedict of Aniane—*MPL,* CIII, 702 ss.

[15] *Regula Canonicorum,* c. XVIII—Luc d'Achery, *Spicilegium,* Vol. I, 569. Also found in *MPL,* LXXXIX, 1067.

[16] *Regula ad Virgines,* Recapitulatio xii—*MPL,* LXVII, 1118.

A. Method of Convoking the Chapter

During this period there was no need of a special way of convoking the chapter because it was a part of the daily horarium and was, therefore, assembled by sounding the common signals.[17] That part of the chapter where the necessary business was discussed was introduced by the superior's saying: *"Loquamur de ordine nostro."*[18] This practice of meeting daily was an advantage for the community in the protection of its rights, for it would be an easy matter to start a discussion if the brethren thought that the abbot was acting beyond his powers.

B. Those Who Had the Right of Suffrage in Chapter

The contemporary literature is not very helpful in the question discussed here. Perhaps the reason this point was never treated directly was that the practice was so well established that it caused no difficulties. A satisfactory answer, however, can be arrived at by way of exclusion.

As has already been seen, St. Benedict in his rule excludes the novices. Paul the Deacon declares that a monk who has committed a grave fault should not be present when the chapter is determining his punishment.[19] A later customary altogether excludes one guilty of grave fault from the chapter.[20] Just after the end of this period a provincial chapter in England, which, since it followed the IV Council of the Lateran (1215), had the force of law for the province,[21] deprived a fugitive who had returned of all suffrage in chapter.[22] The position of lay brothers is not clear but they seem to have been excluded from the time of their institution as a distinct class in the

[17] Martène, *De Antiquis Ecclesiae Ritibus* (4 tom. in 2 vols., Venetiis, 1783), tom. 4, lib. 1, cap. V, IV.

[18] *Statuta Lanfranci*, c. XVIII—*MPL*, CL, 504; *Usus Antiquiores Ordinis Cisterciensis*, c. LXX—*MPL*, CLXVI, 1443-1444.

[19] Page 43.

[20] *Disciplina Farfensis*, c. XV—*MPL*, CL, 1259.

[21] Cf. Article III, Section II, 4, of this chapter.

[22] *Constitutiones Capituli Generalis Provinciae Cantuarensis*—*Monasticon Anglicanum*, Sir William Dugdale, 2. ed., Calley, Ellis and Bandinel, 6 vols in 8 (London, 1817), I, p. xlix.

community, because they were not considered to be monks in the full sense of the word.[23] It may safely be said, then, that all and only those who were what are now called choir monks and who were in good standing had the right to be present and to vote in chapter.

C. Manner of Voting

One thing about which the monastic literature is strangely silent is the manner by which those who had the right of suffrage expressed their vote. The Chronicles of Jocelin show that expression of consent by raising the right hand was used,[24] but whether this was a common practice, or whether there was a common practice, there is no way of knowing in the absence of more conclusive evidence.

D. Matters to Be Treated in Chapter

St. Benedict in legislating for the part of the community in the conduct of the affairs of the monastery prescribed that important matters should be subjected to the advice of the whole community and that less important matters be referred to the seniors alone. In later times the monastic authors list the various matters which come under these categories. In determining what is to be considered an important matter the guiding principle seems to have been like that which we later find formulated in the Rules of Law: "What touches all is to be approved by all." [25] Thus Paul the Deacon says: *"Praecipua est illa res quae ad totam congregationem attinet."* [26] It has already been mentioned that the choice of the abbot belonged to the community. Some of the other matters which should be treated in

[23] Thus Martène (*Commentarium in Regulam S. Benedicti—MPL*, LXVI, 287): ". . . sed neque fratres laici, sive conversi, sive commissi, sive quovis alio nomine vocentur, qui ad exteriora tantum monachorum servitia recepti sunt." He also excludes those incarcerated, excommunicated, interdicted, or suspended; but these would certainly come under the general designation of those who had committed a grave fault.

[24] *Chronica Jocelini—Memorials of St. Edmund's Abbey*, Rolls Series, ed. by Thomas Arnold (2 vols., London, 1890), I, 225.

[25] Reg. 29, R. J. in VI°.

[26] Page 42.

chapter and to which the monastic sources bear witness are: the admission of anyone to the habit and religious profession;[27] the expulsion of a member;[28] penances to be imposed for grave faults;[29] certain acts in the administration of temporal goods;[30] and various appointments.[31]

This list does not pretend to be specific or exhaustive but it is presented merely to give a general yet comprehensive idea of the matters in which the advice of the community was required to be asked.

The less important matters, those on which only the seniors needed to be consulted were those pertaining to the ordinary administration of the monastic officials; e. g., the purchase of clothing, of vessels, etc.,—the obedientiaries as they were called.[32]

E. Nature of the Chapter

As has already been seen, in the chapter as instituted by St. Benedict the community possessed only a consultative suffrage. This was the nature of the community's part in the conduct of the affairs of the monastery almost to the very end of the monastic period.[33] As late as the time of St. Bernard it was at least open to discussion whether the abbot needed the consent of the community for any of

[27] Paul the Deacon, p. 42; *Expositio Regulae ab Hildemaro Tradita,* ed. Mittermueller (Regensburg, 1880), p. 130 (hereafter cited as Hildemar); *Statuta Lanfranci—MPL,* CL, 500-501; *Chronica Jocelini, loc. cit.*

[28] Paul the Deacon, p. 42; Hildemar, p. 130.

[29] Paul the Deacon, p. 43; Hildemar, p. 131.

[30] Hildemar, p. 131; *Chronica Jocelini,* pp. 235, 243; *Provincial Chapter of the Province of Canterbury—Monasticon Anglicanum,* I, p. xlvii.

[31] *Antiquae Consuetudines Insignis Monasterii Sancti Vitoni Virdunensis*—Martène, *De Antiquis Ecclesiae Ritibus* (4 toms. in 2 vols., Venetiis, 1783), tom. IV, p. 300; *Chronica Jocelini,* 225, 322-327; *Chronicon Abbatiae de Evesham,* Rolls Series, ed. by William Dunn MacRay (London, 1863), p. 206.

[32] Paul the Deacon, p. 44; Hildemar, p. 131.

[33] Smaragdus, *Commentaria in Regulam S. Benedicti—MPL,* CII, 745; *Guigonis Carthusiae Maioris Prioris Quinti Consuetudines,* c. XXXVII—*MPL,* CLIII, 713.

his actions.[84] However, toward the end of this period and particularly in the twelfth century various sources bear witness to the trend that the community began to develop as a deliberative body with decisive suffrage in certain matters. Some of the latter are: the admission of a novice to profession;[85] various types of administration and alienation;[86] appointment to monastic benefices and the designation of the major officials of the monastery.[87]

It should be mentioned, however, that the power of the conventual chapter was negative, a power of restriction; that is, it could prevent the abbot from acting in matters where its consent was needed but it could not force him to act. Moreover, there is no evidence of any sanction by which the abbot's action was invalid if he failed to obtain the consent of the brethren.

II. The Provincial and General Chapter

1. *Before the Establishment of the Cistercian Order*

The institution of regional and general chapters among religious really begins with the *Carta Caritatis,* a set of constitutions determining the Cistercian system; but before this there are found several types of assembly which resemble a general chapter and these it is desirable to notice. The very earliest is the annual gathering of the Pachomian monks which has already been discussed. St. Benedict when he established the monastery at Subiaco with its twelve sur-

[84] "Quid? quod abbas statuerit cum consilio seniorum, si non omnes consenseritis? Itane in Regula vestra manifestam super hoc sententiam aut non attenditis aut contemnitis? Mandat siquidem SS. P. N. Benedictus ut fratres ad consilium vocati, singuli sic respondeant quod senserint, quatenus defendere non praesumant quod responderint, sed abbas, auditis singulorum sententiis, quam potissimum ipse elegerit, ei omnes sine contradictione acquiescant."—*Epistolae S. Bernardi,* 397, n. 4—*MPL,* CLXXXII, 608.

[85] *Lanfranci Statuta—MPL,* CL, 500; *Jocelini Chronica,* p. 225.

[86] *Jocelini Chronica,* pp. 235, 243; *Provincial Chapter of the Province of Canterbury—Monasticon Anglicanum,* I, xlvii.

[87] *Jocelini Chronica,* pp. 225, 322-327; *Antiqui Consuetudines Sancti Vitoni*—Martène, *De Antiquis Ritibus Ecclesiae, loc. cit.*; *Gesta Abbatum Sancti Albani,* Rolls Series, ed. Henry Thomas Riley (3 vols., London, 1867-1869), I, 207, 285.

rounding monasteries whose abbots were all appointed by himself [38] may have had the idea of instituting a religious order with a centralized organization, but when he came to write his rule he left no trace of this.

A real regional chapter was the gathering of abbots under St. Benedict of Aniane at Aachen in the year 817. Under an order of Louis the Pious these abbots met for the purpose of introducing complete uniformity into the religious life. The results of their deliberations are to be found in the Capitulary of Aachen,[39] which can well be called the first set of constitutions on the Rule of St. Benedict. This uniformity was to be maintained under St. Benedict as supreme abbot and an inspector was to be placed in each house to see that it was carried out. But, since this gathering really possessed no authority it did not exert any lasting influence; as Cardinal Gasquet says:

> "Such were the plans of Benedict, but they passed like a summer's dream. His scheme of rigid uniformity among the monasteries of the Empire, secured by the appointment of himself as General, aided by an agent or inspector in each house— an idea wholly alien to the most elementary conception of Benedictine life—met with the fate it deserved." [40]

In certain large monasteries there were assemblies of all those who resided in the dependent priories; this was practiced at Monte Cassino in the ninth century,[41] and in the abbey of Marmoutier in the eleventh century.[42] These assemblies were more in the nature of a conventual chapter since dependent priories were considered as part of the motherhouse. These are the principal examples of gatherings greater than conventual chapters before the founding of the Cistercians.

[38] Pope St. Gregory, *Dialogues,* lib. II, 3, 4, 5,—*MPL* LXXVI.

[39] *Capitula Monachorum—Monumenta Germaniae Historica, Leges* (5 vols., I-IV, ed. Pertz; V, ed. Pertz-Waitz-Brunner, Hannoverae, 1835-1889), I, 200-204 (hereafter cited as *MGH, Leges*).

[40] *Preface,* 2. ed. of the English translation of Montalembert, *Monks of the West* (6 vols., New York, 1896), p. xxvi.

[41] Leo Ostiensis, *Chronicon Cassinense,* lib. II, 32—*MPL,* CLXXIII, 531.

[42] Martène, *Thesaurus Anecdotorum,* IV, praef. p. iv.

2. *Among the Cistercians*

The *Carta Caritatis,* which is really the first constitution of the Cistercian Order, was approved by Pope Calixtus II in 1119.[43] In the third chapter it prescribed for a general chapter to be held every year at which all the abbots of the order except those who were sick were to be present.[44] This chapter was to ordain whatever was necessary for the salvation of souls, the observance of the rule and the promotion of peace and charity.[45] The spread of the order to distant countries made it necessary to relax the prescription that all the abbots should come every year and in 1157 the abbots of Scotland received permission to come only every fourth year; the same concession was made to the Irish abbots in the year 1190.

3. *Under the Influence of the Cistercian System*

The Cistercian idea was adopted by other orders. The general chapter was prescribed by the statutes of the Premonstratensians, an order of Canons Regular, whose institute was confirmed by Honorius in 1126. The spread of the Cistercian system to the other religious groups was due principally to Pope Innocent III. Seeing the great good that came to the religious life from these chapters and perhaps realizing that it would be much easier to bring these federated groups under the control of the Holy See, he encouraged and promoted them. His program finally culminated in the twelfth canon of the IV Council of the Lateran (1215) which made these chapters obligatory upon all independent religious houses and with this canon the provincial or regional chapter was introduced into ecclesiastical legislation.

Article II. Chapters in Roman Law

The Roman civil law system was closed too early to permit one to find in it any use of the word chapter. For the purpose of this

[43] Jaffé, *Regesta Pontificum Romanorum ab Condita Ecclesia ad Annum post Christum Natum MCXCVIII* (editionem secundam correctam et auctam auspiciis Gulielmi Wattenbach, curaverunt S. Loewenfeld, F. Kaltenbrunner, P. Ewald, Lipsiae, 1885-1888), n. 6795 (hereafter cited as *JL, JK,* or *JE* as Loewenfeld, Kaltenbrunner or Ewald edited the section cited.)

[44] *Carta Caritatis,* c. III—*MPL,* CLXVI, 1380.

[45] *Op. cit.,* 1381.

study what is to be considered is whether the Roman legislator gave to the community any part in the conduct of the affairs of the monastery. This is found to be the case in three matters: the admission of subjects; the election of the superior; and the administration of temporal goods.

As regards the admission of subjects into the community the notice in the law is like a passing reference and possibly means nothing. In the Fifth Novel, treating of the probation of candidates, the legislator says that after they have lived the life for three years and have shown themselves well-fitted and congenial to the other monks they merit the monastic garb and tonsure.[46] This seems to say that the brethren were to have some voice in the admission of subjects, but certainly this law, on another point, was not followed out in its entirety because the Rule of St. Benedict, which was followed almost universally, prescribed only a year's probation.[47]

The election of the superior is treated in the Code and the law declared that no mere succession should determine the superior, but that he who was commended by integrity of life and good morals and whom the whole body of the monks, or the greater part, have thought worthy of it and have elected should be called to the superiorship.[48]

Roman Law treats in many places of the administration of ecclesiastical property, but only in a few places does it give any part to the monastic community. Thus in a Constitution of Anastasius (491-518), which was originally promulgated only for the city of Byzantium but was later incorporated into the Code, alienation was permitted when it was a question of something that was useless or burdensome, but the community had to be present and what pleased

[46] N. (5, 2): "Et dum triennio tota vita permanserint, optimos semetipsos et tolerabiles aliis monachis demonstrantes, hos monachicam promereri vestem atque tonsuram."

[47] C. LVIII, pp. 105-110.

[48] C. (1, 3): ". . . sed quem et vita integra et honesti mores et assidua devotio commendent et totum reliquorum monachorum corpus vel maior eorum pars ad hoc idoneum putaverit et propositis sanctis evangeliis elegerit, eum ad praefecturam vocari."

the majority should be done.[49] In several places in the One Hundred and Twentieth Novel provision is also made for the consent of those living in the house where extraordinary administration takes place.[50] These few places seem to be the only ones where the Roman Law makes any provision for the community to have a part in the conduct of its affairs.

Article III. Chapters in Ecclesiastical Legislation

Section I. The Local Chapter

1. Before the Decree of Gratian

The inner life of the monastic orders did not receive much attention from ecclesiastical legislators in early times and so there are but few places where they confer on the community as a body any rights in regard to the affairs of the monastery. From very early times, however, the choice of the abbot and abbess seems to have been reserved to the monastic community. This is evident from the canon of councils,[51] and from papal documents.[52] This should not lead one to believe that this practice was observed universally and at all times

[49] C. (1, 2), 17: "Huiusmodi enim rerum, quae nullum lucrum propter sterilitatem produnt, sed damnum tribuunt, nec donationem vel alienationem iisdem domibus interdicimus . . . pro monasteriis vero praepositi aliique monachi adesse debent . . . ut quod maiori parti placuerit id obtineat."

[50] N. (120, 6) 2; (120, 7) 1.

[51] Council of Carthage (534)—Hardouin, *Acta conciliorum et epistolae decretales ac constitutiones summorum pontificum* (12 vols., Parisiis, 1715), II, 1177 (hereafter cited as Hardouin); Lateran Synod (601)—Hardouin, III, 538-539; Council of Chelsea (787), c. v.—*Councils and Ecclesiastical Documents Relating to Great Britain and Ireland*, ed. Haddan and Stubbs (3 vols., Oxford, 1869-1871), III, 450 (hereafter cited as Haddan and Stubbs); Council of Frankfort (794), c. xvii—Hardouin, IV, 903; Council of Rheims (813), c. xxiv —Mansi, *Sacrorum conciliorum nova et amplissima collectio* (53 vols. in 59, Paris, Arnhem, Leipzig, 1901-1927), XIII, 79 (hereafter cited as Mansi); Council of Chelsea, c. iv—Haddan and Stubbs, III, 580-581.

[52] E. g., Gregory the Great, *"Luminosus,"* 6 iun. 595—*JE*, 1362; *Petitionem tuam,"* 6 iun. 595—*JE*, 1363; *"Piae Postulatio voluntatis,"* nov. 596—*JE*, 1458; Formosus, *"Quanto nos piorum,"* 25 nov. 891—*JL*, 3474; John XIII, *"Si piis votis,"* 1 ian. 968—*JL*, 3721.

for it quite definitely was not. In some communities the abbot appointed his successor; in places where the monastery was under the jurisdiction of the bishop, the latter appointed the abbot; and abbeys along with other ecclesiastical benefices were subjected to the abuses of lay-proprietorship. Even in the same place the practice varied.[53]

The only other point in which the legislation during this period gave some right to the brethren was in the administration of the monastic property and these enactments are scarce indeed. The seventh canon of the council of Chelsea in England (816) decreed that the consent and permission of the monastic family was necessary to give away part of the monastic estates.[54] In like manner a decree of Pope Nicholas II declared that it was not lawful for the abbot to alienate or to place under obligation any ecclesiastical goods without the permission and signature of the convent.[55] In 1106 the council of Vastalla decreed that none of the possessions of the Church could be sold, commuted, lent, or given in fief by the abbot without the common consent of the brethren or the bishop of the place.[56]

2. In the Decree of Gratian

Although Gratian has incorporated into his work the method of election established by St. Benedict in his Rule,[57] he does not seem to have considered it as applying to religious except in so far as it determined a common form of election, since it is contained in the Distinction treating of the election of bishops. In the sixteenth Cause a decree of Boniface, the source of which is uncertain, is cited which declared that if the abbot wishes to transfer the monastery from one site to another he must take counsel of the bishop and the brethren.[58] Gratian treated the question of the election of the abbot in the eighteenth Cause and declared that although the IV Council

[53] Thus Knowles (*The Monastic Order in England,* p. 401) divides the years from 800-1200 into six periods in which the appointment of the abbot ranged from designation by the king to free election by the community.

[54] Haddan and Stubbs, III, 582.

[55] Decreta Nicolai II, xv—Mansi, XIX, 876.

[56] Mansi, XX, 1211.

[57] C. 14, D. LXI (*Regula S. Benedicti,* c. LXIV, pp. 117-118).

[58] C. 41, C. XVI, q. 7.

of Toledo (633) provided that only bishops could institute the abbot and other officials,[59] according to Pope Gregory and Pope Pelagius, the congregation of the monastery should institute the abbot,[60] explaining that the decree of the Council of Toledo was passed for stiff-necked monks such as those who tried to kill St. Benedict.[61]

3. In the Decretals of Gregory IX

The development in ecclesiastical legislation between the Decree of Gratian and the promulgation of the Decretals of Gregory IX (1234) which most affected the religious chapter was the great advance in regard to canonical elections. This matter is treated in the fifth and sixth titles of the first book of the Decretals. While the regulations there laid down applied also to the elections conducted in the chapters of religious it would enlarge this study too much if an attempt were made to investigate the historical development of canonical elections.[62]

The right of the monastic chapter to elect the abbot and abbess, though never stated expressly, is presumed in the Decretals. This, for example, can be seen in decretals of Alexander III,[63] Celestine III,[64] and Innocent III.[65] It can also be concluded that at times conventual priors also were elected by the chapter since the Decretals cite a canon of the III Council of the Lateran (1179) that conventual

[59] C. I, C. XVIII, q. 2 (IV Council of Toledo, c. 51—Hardouin, III, 585).

[60] C. 2, 3, 4, C. XVIII, q. 2 (Gregory the Great, *"Luminosus,"* 6 iun. 595—*JE*, 1362; Pelagius I, *"Abbatem in,"* 558-560—*JK*, 987).

[61] Dictum post c. 8, C. XVIII, q. 2.

[62] Cf. Parsons, *Canonical Elections* (Catholic University of America Canon Law Studies: No. 118, Washington: Catholic University of America Press, 1939), Part One, Historical Synopsis (hereafter cited as Parsons, *Canonical Elections*).

[63] C. 8, X, *de electione et electi potestate*, I, 6 (*"Causam quae inter,"* 1159-1181—*JL*, 14070).

[64] C. 13, X, *de electione et electi potestate*, I, 6 (*"Cum monasterium de,"* 1191-1198—*JL*, 17617).

[65] C. 16, 38, X, *de electione et electi potestate*, I, 6 (*"Cum inter dilectum,"* 7 apr. 1199; *"Officii tui laudabilem,"* 1209—Potthast, *Regesta Pontificum Romanorum inde ab anno post Christum natum MCXCVIII ad annum MCCCIV* [2 vols., Berolini, 1874-1875], 1657, 3660 [hereafter cited as Potthast]).

priors canonically elected by the chapter are not to be removed without cause.[66]

A decretal of Celestine III reserved to the chapter the right of presenting someone for a church when the right of making such a presentation pertained to a collegiate church. If this presentation was made without the consent of the majority of the collegiate chapter the provision was of no force, unless there was a contrary custom or privilege conferring this right of presentation on the superior alone.[67] Under provision of the Decretals, before a superior could perform any act of extraordinary temporal administration he needed the consent of the chapter. This was established by decretals of Alexander III [68] and by a canon of the IV Council of the Lateran (1215).[69] A right not possessed by the chapter from the law in the Decretals was that of deposing the abbot, for in a constitution of Honorius III this right was given to the bishop in non-exempt monasteries, while in an exempt monastery it was reserved to the Apostolic See.[70] In this same constitution Honorius decreed that secular clerics who had received a prebend in the monastery had no right of suffrage in chapter.[71] A canon of the III Council of the Lateran, incorporated in the Decretals, decreed that it was the will of the majority in chapter which was to prevail.[72]

[66] C. 2, X, *de statu monachorum et canonicorum regularium,* III, 35 (III Council of the Lateran, c. 10—Mansi, XXII, 224). There are two kinds of priors, conventual and claustral. The former were superiors of priories; the latter second in authority to the abbot in the abbey.

[67] C. 6, X, *de his quae fiunt a Praelatis sine capitulo,* III, 10 (*"Ea noscitur Sedis,"* 1191-1198—*JL,* n. 17644).

[68] C. 2, 3, X, *de donationibus,* III, 24 (*"Fraternitatem tuam credimus,"* 1178-1181; *"Ceterum si abbatem,"* 1163-1179—*JL,* nn. 14330, 13162); c. 2, 3, X, *de his quae fiunt a Praelatis sine capitulo,* III, 10 (*"Continebatur in litteris,"* 1159-1181; *"Cum iam nos pridem,"* 1163-1178—*JL,* nn. 14033, 13164).

[69] C. 4, X, *de fideiussoribus,* III, 22 (c. 59—Mansi, XXII, 1047).

[70] C. 8, X, *de statu monachorum et canonicorum regularium,* III, 35 (*"Ea quae pro,"* 13 sept. 1225—Potthast, n. 7817).

[71] *Loc. cit.*

[72] C. 1, X, *de his quae fiunt a maiori parte capituli,* III, 11 (c. 16—Mansi, XXII, 227).

It is evident from some of the decretals that have already been mentioned that failure to obtain the consent of the chapter when it was required by law invalidated the act of the superior.[73]

4. In Particular Conciliar Legislation

The Council of Paris (1212) provided for a council of seven seniors elected by the majority of the chapter with whom the abbot had to consult before he undertook any important business or borrowed large sums of money.[74] This same council required the abbot to render an account of his administration to this council of seniors,[75] and in the seventeenth canon it forbade the abbot or prior, unless he had consulted the chapter, to threaten or do anything to one who had proposed something for the correction of the house or the prior.[76] The Council of Melun (1216) ordered the abbot to make an account of his administration, in chapter, annually.[77] In the sixth canon this council prohibited the abbot from borrowing money, beyond the sum established by the bishop, without the consent of the chapter.[78]

Section II. The Provincial and the General Chapter

As has already been said the spread of the Cistercian idea of the general chapter to the other monastic groups is due principally to the influence of Innocent III. Papal approbation of the constitutions of the Cistercians and the Premonstratensians made these a matter of ecclesiastical legislation for these particular institutes, but even though Innocent III by his letters ordered or approved these chapters for other places from time to time, they were not required by any general legislation until he had assembled the IV General Council of the Lateran (1215). The twelfth canon of this council is the first general law making these chapters obligatory upon all religious houses.[79] This

[73] E.g., c. 2, 3, 6, X, *de his quae fiunt a Praelatis sine capitulo,* III, 10.
[74] Pars III, c. xv—Mansi, XXII, 837.
[75] *Loc. cit.*
[76] Mansi, XXII, 838.
[77] C. v—Mansi, XXII, 1088.
[78] *Loc. cit.*
[79] Mansi, XXII, 999.

canon was incorporated into the Decretals of Gregory IX.[80] Since it is the foundation of all later legislation on the general and provincial chapter, the writer has thought it advisable to quote it here and then give a very brief commentary on it.

"In every ecclesiastical province there shall be held every three years, saving the right of the diocesan ordinaries, a general chapter of abbots and of priors having no abbots, who have not been accustomed to celebrate such chapters. This shall be held in a monastery best adapted to this purpose and shall be attended by all who are not canonically impeded, with this restriction, however, that no one bring with him more than six horses and eight persons. In inaugurating this new arrangement, let two neighboring abbots of the Cistercian order be invited to give them counsel and opportune assistance, since among them the celebration of such chapters is of long standing. These two Cistercians shall without hindrance choose from those present two whom they consider the most competent, and these four shall preside over the entire chapter, so that no one of these four may assume the authority of leadership; should it become expedient, they may be changed by prudent deliberation. Such a chapter shall be celebrated for several consecutive days according to the custom of the Cistercian order. During its deliberations careful attention is to be given to the reform of the order and to regular observance, and what has been enacted with the approval of the four shall be observed inviolably by all, excuses, contradictions, and appeals to the contrary notwithstanding. In each of these chapters the place for the holding of the following one is to be determined. All those in attendance, even if for want of room many must occupy other houses, must live the *vita communis* and bear proportionately all common expenses. In the same chapter religious and prudent persons should be appointed who, in our name, shall visit every abbey in the province, not only of monks but also of nuns, according to a form prescribed for them, correcting and reforming those things that need correction and reform; so that, if they should know that the rector of a locality ought to be removed from office, let them make it known to his bishop, that he may procure his removal; but if he should neglect to do it, then the appointed visitors shall refer the matter to the attention of the Apostolic See. We wish and command that canons regular observe this according to their order. But if in this new arrangement a difficulty should arise which cannot be disposed of by

[80] C. 7, X, *de statu monachorum et canonicorum regularium,* III, 35.

the aforesaid persons, let it be referred without scandal to the judgment of the Apostolic See; in the meantime let the other things that have been accomplished by amicable deliberation be inviolably observed. Moreover, the diocesan ordinaries must strive so to reform the monasteries subject to them, that when the aforesaid visitors come to them they will find in them more that is worthy of commendation than of correction, taking special care lest the monasteries be oppressed by them with undue burdens. For, while we wish that the rights of the superiors be respected, we do not on that account wish that injury be sustained by inferiors. We strictly command diocesan bishops and persons attending the chapters, that with ecclesiastical censure—every appeal being denied—they restrain advocates, patrons, vicegerents, rulers, consuls, nobles, and soldiers, and all others, from molesting the monasteries either in persons or properties and if perchance these persons should so molest, let the aforesaid bishops and chapter members not neglect to compel these latter to make satisfaction, that the monasteries may serve Almighty God more freely and peacefully." [81]

1. Convocation

This canon did not decree any special manner of convocation. This was probably thought to be unnecessary since it did provide that the chapter should be held every three years and that the preceding chapter was to determine the place where the next chapter would be held.

2. Persons Constituting the Chapter

The chapter prescribed by this canon, even though the establishing of it was inspired by the general chapter of the Cistercians, was not a general chapter in the sense that the Cistercian chapter was called general, that is, representative of a whole religious order. This chapter was confined within the boundaries of some province or kingdom. All the abbots and conventual priors residing in the province or kingdom in which the chapter was held and who did not have such chapters in their own order were obliged to be present at this chapter unless they were prevented by some canonical impediment. The

[81] Translation from Schroeder, *Disciplinary Decrees of the General Councils: Text, Translation, and Commentary* (St. Louis: B. Herder Book Co., 1937), pp. 253-254.

canon prescribed these chapters for the orders of canons regular as well as for the monastic orders.

3. Presiding Officers

In order to prevent anyone from assuming the authority of leadership the canon prescribed that four abbots were to preside. In the beginning, two of these abbots were to be Cistercians, invited for that purpose, because from their longstanding custom they were experienced in the manner of conducting these chapters. These two were to choose two others. How these four abbots were to be chosen, after the presence of the Cistercian abbots was no longer necessary, was not determined in the canon. Probably it was left to the chapter to determine the way in which they were to be selected.

4. Power of the Chapter

The chapter clearly possessed complete power of jurisdiction for it had power to legislate, and against its enactments there was no appeal. Moreover, it was given power to enforce its regulations through its right to appoint canonical visitors. In a later constitution it received power to suspend an abbot from his office, but not the power to depose him.[82]

5. The Competence of the Chapter

The chapter had the right to legislate for all things which concerned the reform of the order and regular discipline. It determined the place of the next chapter, appointed canonical visitors, and was authorized to restrain anyone, even with canonical censures, from molesting the monasteries either in person or property and to compel anyone who had infringed the rights of the monastery to make satisfaction.

[82] Honorius III, "*Ea quae pro,*" 13 sept. 1225—Potthast, n. 7817. This constitution is found in the Decretals—c. 8, X, *de statu monachorum et canonicorum regularium,* III, 35.

Summary

From what has been said so far it is quite clear that, before the Rule of St. Benedict, except for the election of the abbot which in a few places was a right possessed by the community, the brethren of the monastery had no voice in the conduct of its affairs, but that everything was in the exclusive control of the abbot. St. Benedict, while reserving the right of choosing the abbot to the whole community, did not curtail the supreme power of the abbot in other matters; but, convinced that he would rule wisely only if he took counsel, provided that in all things the abbot should ask advice before acting. The right of decision, however, remained solely with the abbot. Gradually the custom was introduced that the superior must obtain not only the advice but also the consent of the brethren in some of the important matters. But there is no evidence in the monastic literature of a sanction invalidating the action of the abbot if he failed to obtain this consent. The sanction was the contribution of canon law to the development of the chapter when the chapter's prerogatives began to pass over from community customs into ecclesiastical legislation. The final transition from custom to written law was not made even at the end of the Monastic Era. But during this time occurred the gradual development of the community chapter into a corporate body possessing deliberative and decisive rights.

The tendency of the monastic communities to unite in general assemblies to promote good order and necessary reforms is evident as early as the time of St. Pachomius. All attempts at permanent union directed toward the attaining of this purpose ended in failure during the greater part of the Monastic Era. It was only with the establishment of the Cistercian order in the twelfth century that these general chapters were permanently instituted. From them the idea spread to other orders, principally through the efforts of Innocent III. It was finally through him that the were imposed on all monasteries and canons regular by the IV Council of the Lateran. This Council conferred on them legislative power in regard to all things concerning the reform of the order and the regular discipline and gave them an appropriate means to enforce their statutes in their right to appoint canonical visitors.

CHAPTER III

THE MENDICANT ERA

ARTICLE I. CHAPTERS IN THE MENDICANT ORDERS

THE most noteworthy contributions of the Mendicant orders to the government of religious societies were organization and representation. The monastic orders were distinguished by the independence of every house and the stability of residence of the members in a particular house. The Mendicant orders abandoned both of these ideas. To them the members were members of an order which was world wide and which was ruled by a centralized government elected by the members or their representatives. Another change introduced into the system of government of religious societies by the Mendicant orders was a provincial chapter which was based upon the division of the order itself into provinces and not confined within the boundaries of some province or kingdom as was the chapter prescribed by the IV Council of the Lateran. This whole system of government reached its full development first in the Order of Preachers. The earliest Constitutions of the Dominicans (1228) contain, at least in embryo, every type of collegiate body now found in religious institutes: the local chapter and council; the provincial chapter and council; and the general chapter and council.[1] Since this represents the final stage in the development of religious chapters a brief description of them as portrayed in these Constitutions will not be out of place.

These early Constitutions did not specify which members of the community had the right to be present in the local chapter, but a new edition made by St. Raymond of Peñafort (1240) provided that two years after profession and one year after transfer from another province the brethren were to be admitted to the local chapter (dist. II,

[1] These Constitutions were edited by Denifle—*Archiv für Literatur—und Kirchengeschichte des Mittelalters,* ed. by Ehrle-Denifle (7 vols., Berlin-Freiburg im Breisgau, 1885-1890), I, (Berlin, 1895), 165-227.

c. 2).[2] The local chapter elected the conventual prior (dist. II, 24), the local council (dist. II, 35), and its representatives to the provincial chapter (dist. II, 1, 15). Its consent was necessary for the admission of candidates and with its counsel three brethren were chosen by the superior to examine these candidates (dist. I, 14). The local council had to be consulted for any building project (dist. II, 35) and for the appointment of the subprior (dist. II, 25).

The provincial chapter was composed of the provincial prior (dist. II, 4), the conventual priors of the province, the two representatives elected by each house, and the preachers general of the province (dist. II, 1).[3] This chapter had the right to elect the provincial prior (dist. II, 15), the *definitores* of the provincial chapter (dist. II, 1), a *definitor* of the general chapter (dist. II, 5), two brethren to represent the province in the election of the Master General (dist. II, 10), and four brethren to fulfill the office of visitors (dist. II, 19). It approved those who were fit for preaching (dist. II, 20). No new statute could be made by the chapter until it had been approved by three successive chapters, a measure laid down to prevent excessive multiplication of legislation (dist. II, 6).

The four *definitores* of the provincial chapter were not what are understood today as provincial councillors since their office existed only during the time of the chapter, but they bear a striking resemblance to them and may be the source of this institution. Together with the provincial prior they discussed and settled all matters (dist. II, 2), and determined the place where the next chapter would be held (dist. II, 4). Moreover, they heard and corrected all complaints brought in chapter against the provincial prior and in case of incorrigibility could suspend him from office until the time of the general chapter (dist. II, 3).

There seems to have been a twofold general chapter; the ordinary one which met every year, and one which met whenever there was need to elect the Master General. The ordinary general chapter was

[2] Denifle also edited this edition of St. Raymond—*Archiv für Literatur- und Kirchengeschichte des Mittelalters,* V (Freiburg im Breisgau, 1889), 530-564.

[3] "Praedicatores autem generales dicimus, qui per priorem provincialem et diffinitores capituli provincialis fuerint instituti."—Edition of St. Raymond of Peñafort, dist. II, c. 7.

composed of the Master General and one *definitor* elected by the provincial chapter of each province (dist. II, 5). The provincial chapter of the province where this general chapter was being held was required to come to it, there being no need to hold another chapter in that province the same year (dist. II, 9). The chapter for the election of the Master General was composed of the provincial priors and two brethren elected by the provincial chapters. After they had assembled they were inclosed in conclave which they could not leave until they had elected the Master General. No food was given them meanwhile (dist. II, 10). The matters that came within the competence of the general chapter seem to have been the same respecting the whole order as those within the competence of the provincial chapter respecting the province.

The general *definitores* together with the Master General discussed and settled all matters. The correction of the Master General was in their hands, and apparently they could even depose him from office. Before they did this, however, they were obliged to attempt to induce him to resign (dist. II, 7, 8, 9).

Briefly, this was the system of organization which St. Dominic established for his religious. Much of it did not originate with him but he gave it the final form.[4] With the progress of time it came to be followed in its general outlines by the other Mendicant orders and by many of the congregations of simple vows that were established after the Council of Trent. Even the older monastic orders adopted it in some measure; for example, the Benedictine Congregations which were to be formed about two centuries later resembled very strikingly the Dominican province. Since there are no other noteworthy developments to be found in later religious foundations,

[4] Barker (*The Dominican Order and Convocation,* Oxford, 1913) discusses the possible dependence of the Dominican system upon the Premonstratensians, the Military Orders, the Franciscans and the civil systems of Spain and Southern France. In this small book (82 pages) he also treats of the influence of the Dominicans upon later religious institutes, episcopal synods in England and civil representative government. For more recent treatment of the same subject, cf.: Mandonnet, *Saint Dominique* (2 vols., Paris: Desclée, 1938), II, 103-273; Scheeben, "Die Konstitutionen des Dominikanerordens unter Jordan von Sachsen"—*Quellen und Forschungen zur Geschichte des Dominikanerordens in Deutschland* (Leipzig, 1907—), fasc. 38 (1938).

this study will now be confined solely to the ecclesiastical legislation affecting religious chapters.

Article II. Chapters in Ecclesiastical Legislation

1. *In the Decretal Law of the Liber Sextus and the Clementines*

The decretal law in the Liber Sextus (1298) and the Clementines (1317) determined the personnel of religious chapters in a negative way by ruling out certain classes. Thus decretals of Boniface VIII in the Liber Sextus excluded non-professed from participation in elections with professed religious, lay *conversi* from participation in elections with clerical religious,[5] and a nun under twelve years of age from participation in the election of the abbess.[6] A constitution of Clement V, promulgated in the Council of Vienne (1311-1312) and incorporated in the Clementines, excluded from the chapter a mendicant who had passed to a non-mendicant order even with the permission of the Apostolic See.[7] Another decretal of Boniface in the Liber Sextus determined that two-thirds of those having the right of suffrage was sufficient to constitute a quorum.[8]

In the Rules of Law contained in the Liber Sextus the principle was laid down: "What touches all is to be approved by all," [9] this can well be called one of the principles which determined the matters which were in the competence of the chapter and it is listed among the sources which Cardinal Gasparri gives for canon 526. This canon gives to all members of a community of religious women the right of suffrage where there is question of retaining the ordinary confessor. The extraordinary administration of temporal goods continued in these later sources to be listed as requiring the consent of the chapter. Examples of legislation on this point are a canon of the II Council of Lyons (1274) incorporated in the Liber Sextus [10] and

[5] C. 32, *de electione et electi potestate,* I, 6, in VI°.

[6] C. 43, *de electione et electi potestate,* I, 6, in VI°.

[7] C. 1, *de regularibus et transeuntibus ad religionem,* III, 9, in Clem.

[8] C. 43, *de electione et electi potestate,* I, 6, in VI°.

[9] Reg. 29, R. J., in VI°.

[10] C. 2, *de rebus Ecclesiae non alienandis,* III, 9, in VI°.

a decretal of Clement V found in the Clementines.[11] A decretal of Boniface VIII in the Liber Sextus seems to be the first universal law which dealt with the right of the chapter respecting the admission of subjects. In this decretal Boniface decided that, when the abbey was left vacant by the death of the abbot, the convent could not receive any new members if the right of admitting belonged to the abbot alone, but if the right belonged at the same time to both the abbot and the convent then the convent could admit new members.[12] It is clear that this decretal merely recognized whatever right the chapter already possessed in this matter and conferred no new power on it. A decretal of Boniface VIII did introduce a new provision when it declared that the counsel of the convent was needed before any of the members could be sent to study at a university.[13] Clement V, in the Council of Vienne, decided that when the abbot who had the right to confer benefices was suspended from the exercise of this right it devolved upon the claustral prior and the chapter.[14]

The provincial and general chapters, so far as can be ascertained, were mentioned only twice in these decretals. The prescription of the IV Council of the Lateran that provincial chapters were to be held every three years was repeated by Clement V in the Council of Vienne and included in the Clementines.[15] In the same council Clement V settled a dispute which had arisen among the Franciscans as to whom the right belonged to elect the provincial minister by decreeing that this right belonged to the provincial chapter.[16]

2. *In Legislation From Other Sources*

In the V Council of the Lateran it was decreed that temporary pacts made between regulars and the bishops were valid unless abolished by the subsequent general or provincial chapter.[17] The par-

[11] C. 1, *de rebus Ecclesiae non alienandis,* III, 4, in Clem.

[12] C. 6, *de regularibus et transeuntibus ad religionem,* III, 14, in VI°.

[13] C. 2, *ne clerici vel monachi saecularibus negotiis se immisceant,* III, 24, in VI°.

[14] C. 1, *de statu monachorum et canonicorum regularium,* III, 10, in Clem.

[15] C. 1, *de statu monachorum et canonicorum regularium,* III, 10, in Clem.

[16] C. 1, *de verborum significatione,* V, 11, in Clem.

[17] Sess. XI, 7—Hardouin, IX, 1833.

ticular councils of this period added no new provisions to the legislation already enacted but continued to follow the trend already established. They were principally concerned with the administration of the temporalities. Noteworthy, however, in the acts of particular councils are decrees enforcing the canon of the IV Council of the Lateran that provincial chapters be held.[18]

The papal legislation after the Clementines seems to have been mostly of a particular nature, that is, directed to particular groups. Thus in 1336 a bull of Benedict XII, commonly called the *Benedictina,* ordered three kinds of chapters for the Benedictines—general, provincial and particular.[19] This bull led to the forming of the Benedictine Congregations which were very much like the provinces of the mendicants except that each was entirely independent. One of these, the Congregation of St. Justina, was approved by a bull of Eugene IV in 1432 [20] and may be cited as exemplifying the others. In this bull the pope laid down directions for the conduct of chapters which became a guide for all Benedictine Congregations whether established before or after the Council of Trent.[21]

Summary

From what has been said in this chapter it can be seen that the principal development during the era of the Mendicants was the in-

[18] E. g.: Council of Cologne (1248), c. xx—Mansi, XXIII, 768; Council of Salzburg (1274), c. i—Mansi, XXIV, 136-137; Council of Salzburg (1281), c. vii—Mansi, XXIV, 399.

[19] Benedict XII, *"Summi Magistri,"* 20 iun. 1336, I, III, V—*Bullarum Diplomatum et Privilegiorum Sanctorum Pontificum Taurinensis Editio,* auspicante Cardinali Francisco Gaude (25 vols., Augustae Taurinorum, 1857-1872), V, 348, 352, 356 (hereafter cited as *Bull. Rom. Taur.*). The general chapter mentioned in this bull is not the general chapter of the Benedictines as it is known today. The former was an assembly composed of the abbot of the motherhouse and the priors of the dependent priories. The Benedictine general chapter of today dates only to the time of Leo XIII at the close of the nineteenth century. Cf. Butler, *Benedictine Monachism,* 258 ff.

[20] *"Etsi ex solicitudinis,"* 23 nov. 1432—*Bull. Rom. Taur.*, VI, 11-15.

[21] Calmét, *Commentaire,* pref. p. 59. The historical development of the Benedictine organization is given by Butler, *Benedictine Monachism,* in the chapter "Benedictine Polity," pp. 234-257.

troduction by the Mendicant orders of a centralized representative system of government. The common law did not add much to what it had already enacted, but merely added certain qualifications which had to be possessed in order to have the right of suffrage and specified a few matters for which the counsel or consent of the chapter was necessary.

CHAPTER IV

THE ERA OF MODERN CONGREGATIONS

The time between the Council of Trent and the promulgation of the Code of Canon Law saw the rise of many congregations of simple vows. These were not considered to be religious societies in the sense that the regular orders were [1] and, consequently, the law for regulars did not apply to them.

The present chapter will treat first the legislation of the Council of Trent that was applicable to religious chapters, then a general portrayal of chapters as they existed in the regular orders from the Council of Trent to the present Code, and finally a short discussion of chapters in congregations of simple vows.

Article I. Chapters in the Tridentine Legislation

The Council of Trent by increasing the age for profession to sixteen years for all religious, both men and women,[2] automatically increased the age at which the religious was given the right of suffrage in chapter since the law already provided that only professed religious could have the right of suffrage. The Council recognized the right of the bishop to dispense from this in the case of a girl over twelve but under sixteen years of age.[3] If a bishop granted this dispensation there seems to be no reason why one so dispensed should not have the right of suffrage. In clerical institutes one had to have at least the order of subdiaconate to have the right of suffrage.[4] While it is true that in stating the latter qualification the Council of Trent was considering chapter of churches, its provision in this

[1] Berutti, *Institutiones Iuris Canonici,* Vol. III, *De Religiosis* (Romae: Marietti, 1936), p. 8, note (7) (hereafter cited as Berutti, *De Religiosis*).

[2] Sess. XXV, *de regularibus,* c. 15.

[3] Sess. XXV, *de regularibus,* c. 17.

[4] Sess. XXII, *de ref.,* c. 4.

regard was understood to apply also to conventual chapters. This conclusion is confirmed from a declaration made to the Capuchins that lay brothers might be admitted to the chapter *"non obstante concilio Tridentino."* [5] According to the council those who had been convicted of violation of the vow of poverty by the exercise of proprietorship were to be deprived of active and passive suffrage for two years.[6] In order to safeguard the freedom of election in chapter the Council decreed that secret ballots had to be used and declared that the superior had no right to supply the votes of absent members.[7]

As regards provincial chapters it ordered that, in accordance with the constitution of Innocent III, all monasteries which were not subject to such chapters should establish such congregations within a year after the closing of the Council. If these monasteries proved negligent in this matter, the metropolitans were required to see to it that this prescription was carried out. Should it so happen that there were not enough monasteries in the province to form such a congregation, then two or three provinces were required to form one congregation and it was granted the same power as the chapter in other orders.[8] Those chapters which had the right to delegate persons to supervise monasteries of nuns were authorized by the Council to continue doing so.[9] The Council ordered that all superiors in chapter, provincial or general, should see to it that the members regulated their lives according to the rule they had professed, especially in regard to those things which pertained to the perfection of their profession, and declared they were not authorized to make any relaxation in those things which pertained to the substance of the regular life.[10]

[5] *Bullarium Ordinis Fratrum Minorum Capucinorum,* ed. a Michaele a Tugio in Helvetia (7 vols., Romae, 1740-1752), I, 103 (hereafter cited as *Bullarium Capucinorum*).

[6] Sess. XXV, *de regularibus,* c. 2.

[7] Sess. XXV, *de regularibus,* c. 6.

[8] Sess. XXV, *de regularibus,* c. 8.

[9] Sess. XXV, *de regularibus,* c. 9.

[10] Sess. XXV, *de regularibus,* c. 1.

Article II. Chapters in the Orders of Regulars

I. *The Local Chapter*

The common law never established any definite provisions about the convocation of the local chapter. Naturally it would be convoked by the superior who would preside and this in most cases would be the local superior, and he would convoke it at those times when matters in which it had a right to be heard were to be decided.[11]

In like manner the determination of which members of the community had the right of suffrage in the local chapter was never made by common law but depended on the constitutions of each institute.[12] Common law did provide some restrictions and explanations. Thus in an institute of solemn vows which required the expiration of a determined number of years from religious profession before the religious would have the right of suffrage, this time, according to a declaration of the Sacred Congregation on the Religious state, was to be computed from the first profession, that is, the profession of simple vows,[13] with this restriction, that if the local chapter had a right to be heard in regard to admission to solemn profession, members in simple vows could take no part in this discussion.[14] It is quite evident that if a canonical election was to be conducted in chapter, only those who fulfilled all the requirements of an elector could have the right of suffrage in the chapter, saving always, of course, particular

[11] Piatus Montensis, *Praelectiones Iuris Regularis* (3. ed., 2 vols., Tornaci, 1906), I, 654, 662 (hereafter cited as Piat, *Praelectiones*); Bachofen, *Compendium Iuris Regularium* (New York: Benziger, 1903), p. 258 (hereafter cited as Bachofen, *Compendium*); Vermeersch, *De Religiosis,* I, n. 406, 3; Wernz, *Ius Decretalium,* Tom. III (Romae, 1908), n. 696, III (hereafter cited as Wernz, *Ius Decretalium*).

[12] Vermeersch, *De Religiosis,* I, n. 403, 5; Wernz, *loc. cit.*

[13] S. C. super Statu Regularium, decl., 12 iun. 1858, VIII—*Codicis Iuris Canonici Fontes cura Emi. Petri Card. Gasparri editi,* 9 vols. (Romae [later Civitate Vaticana]: Typis Polyglottis Vaticanis, 1923-1939), (Vols. VII, VIII, IX, ed. cura et studio Emi. Iustiniani Card. Serédi), n. 4383 (hereafter cited as *Fontes*); S. C. Ep. et Reg., decr., *"Perpensis,"* 3 maii 1902, n. 8—*Fontes,* n. 2039.

[14] S. C. super Statu Regularium, 7 febr. 1862—*Fontes,* n. 4387; S. C. Ep. et Reg., decr., *"Perpensis,"* 3 maii 1902, n. 8—*Fontes,* n. 2039.

constitutions and privileges.[15] All the members of a community of women religious were declared to have the right of suffrage when there was question of retaining the ordinary confessor.[16] A woman who entered an institute in which two of her sisters were already members was declared to lack active and passive suffrage.[17] Authors were not agreed regarding the extension of the penalty of deprivation of suffrage inflicted by common law to other matters besides elections.[18]

As has already been said, ordinarily the local chapter was presided over by the local superior, but this was a question to be decided according to the constitutions and statutes of each institute. In chapters of nuns for the election of the superioress the bishop presided.[19]

For the most part the matters in which the counsel or consent of the local chapter was needed and also the nature of the competence possessed by the chapter were determined by the particular laws of each institute. In regard to the reception of novices and admission to profession, authors before the Code were not in agreement as to whether the chapter had competence in this matter from common law.[20] The fact that there was disagreement seems to indicate that there was no prescription of common law that was universally binding. There was such a prescription for Italy and the adjacent islands.[21] The pre-Code authors in treating this question say that it was commonly admitted that in communities of nuns this was a right pertaining to the local chapter from common law, but they

15 Thus the Capuchin order obtained a declaration that lay brothers might be admitted to chapter "non obstante concilio Tridentino."—*Bullarium Capucinorum*, I, 103.

16 S. C. de Religiosis, decr., 3 febr. 1913, n. 2 (b)—*Fontes*, n. 4416.

17 S. C. Ep. et Reg., 3 iun. 1701—*Collectanea in Usum Secretariae Sacrae Congregationis Episcoporum et Regularium*, ed. A. Bizzarri (Romae, 1885), p. 336 (hereafter cited as Bizzarri).

18 Cf. Piat, *Praelectiones*, II, 610.

19 Gregory XV, const., "*Inscrutabili Dei providentia*," 5 febr. 1622, § 5—*Bull. Rom. Taur.*, XII, 657.

20 Bachofen, *Compendium*, pp. 89-90; Piat, *Praelectiones*, I, 144; Wernz, *Ius Decretalium*, III, n. 643.

21 S. C. super Statu Regularium, decr., "*Regulari Disciplinae*," 25 ian. 1848, Pars Secunda, III—*Fontes*, n. 4367.

cite no law upon which this right was founded.[22] The vote of the chapter, wherever it was required for admission to solemn profession, was merely consultative.[23]

In the year 1909 the Sacred Congregation for Religious issued an instruction requiring the consent of the general, provincial or local council for certain extraordinary acts of administration of temporal goods. This instruction left in force any more stringent regulations of particular constitutions. If by such constitutions the consent of the local chapter was required, it seems it would still be required even after the issuance of this instruction. This instruction prescribed the establishment of these councils for all institutes which did not already have them. In houses *sui iuris* the councillors were to be elected by the free deliberative suffrage of the local chapter.[24]

II. *The Provincial Chapter*

Practically every point concerning the convocation of the provincial chapter—the manner, the time, the place, the frequency, the superior who had the right to convoke it and to preside, the persons who had a right to be called—were determined by the particular law for each institute.[25] The prescription of the IV Council of the Lateran that these chapters should meet at least every three years remained in force.[26]

Most of the powers of the chapter, however, were those derived from common law. Before the Council of Trent the IV Council of the Lateran, as has already been noted, conferred legislative authority on the provincial chapter,[27] and Clement V in the Council of Vienne had declared that the election of the provincial superior was in the power of this chapter.[28] Under legislation promulgated after

[22] Cf. Pellizzarius, *Tractatio de Monialibus* (Romae, 1761), pp. 6, 25; Bachofen, *Compendium*, p. 91; Piat, *Praelectiones*, I, 150; Wernz, *Ius Decretalium*, III, n. 631.

[23] S. C. super Statu Regularium, 7 febr. 1862—*Fontes*, n. 4367; S. C. Ep. et Reg., *Bononien.*, 28 iul. 1902—*Fontes*, n. 2040.

[24] S. C. de Religiosis, instr., *"Inter ea,"* 30 iul. 1909, I, V, X—*Fontes*, n. 4394.

[25] Vermeersch, *De Religiosis*, I, n. 406, 5.

[26] Vermeersch, *De Religiosis*, I, n. 405, 1.

[27] Cf. Vermeersch, *loc. cit.*

[28] C. 1, *de verborum significatione*, V, 11, in Clem.

the Council of Trent this chapter could reserve cases; [29] legitimate the illegitimate; [30] choose three worthy and skilled priests to examine those destined for hearing confession, for preaching and for teaching; [31] and choose the master of novices and his assistant.[32] It should be noted, however, that the rights of the chapter in regard to all these matters could be, and many were, taken away or restricted by the rules, constitutions and privileges which constituted particular law for each order. This particular law could also place other actions within the competence of the provincial chapter.[33]

III. *The General Chapter*

The provisions of common law concerning the general chapter were few. The general chapter, like the provincial chapter, in regard to most of the details was governed by the particular law of each institute. Ordinarily, from the constitutions, the general chapter was convoked by the Superior General, or by him who supplied his place, and he also presided at the celebration of the chapter.[34] An exception to the general rule was the order of Friars Minor. The right to preside in its general chapter belonged to its Cardinal Protector or to a delegate of the Holy See.[35]

The general chapter was the supreme power in the order. Hence, besides being able to do whatever the provincial chapter could do, it could also make statutes or laws which would be binding on the whole order and on the Superior General himself.[36] It could not, however, enact anything contrary to common law, or, according to

[29] S. C. Ep. et Reg., decr., 21 sept. 1624—Bizzarri, 246-247.

[30] Gregory XIV, const., *"Circumspecta,"* 15 mart. 1591, § 4—*Fontes,* n. 170.

[31] Clement VIII, const., *"Nullus omnino,"* 25 iul. 1599, § 24—*Bull. Rom. Taur.,* X, 666.

[32] Clement VIII, const., *"Cum ad regularum,"* 19 mart. 1603, § 9—*Fontes,* n. 189.

[33] Wernz, *Ius Decretalium,* III, n. 696, II; Vermeersch, *De Religiosis,* I, n. 405; Piat, *Praelectiones,* I, 660.

[34] Wernz, *Ius Decretalium,* III, n. 696, I; Vermeersch, *De Religiosis,* I, n. 403, 5; Piat, *Praelectiones,* I, 656-657. Cf. also, Clement IX, const., *"Cum sicut,"* 21 oct. 1669, § 1—*Bull. Rom. Taur.,* XVII, 826.

[35] Piat, *Praelectiones,* I, 657.

[36] Wernz, *Ius Decretalium,* III, n. 696, I; Vermeersch, *De Religiosis,* I, n. 402, 2; Piat, *Praelectiones,* I, 657.

the common opinion, impose any more strict regulation than was required by the rule, since its legislative competence was founded upon the vow of obedience, the obligations of which were assumed according to the rule.[37] According to the general principles governing legislative competence, since it could make these laws or statutes, it could revoke them. But if these statutes were approved by the Holy See in special form they became pontifical law, and so could not be abrogated by the general chapter.

By the provisions of constitutions, universally binding, which were promulgated after the Council of Trent, the general chapter was obliged to choose three religious to pass judgment of expulsion on the incorrigible[38] and to it was to be made a report on the administration of the temporal goods and on the financial condition of the order.[39] Piat says that according to the constitutions of all orders the general chapter elected the Superior General and could punish and depose him.[40] He also raises the question whether the general chapter could found a new province and decides, that saving a special indult, it could not, since this would be establishing quasi-episcopal power and this is reserved to the Holy See.[41]

Article III. Chapters in Congregations of Simple Vows

During the eighteenth and nineteenth centuries there arose in the Church a great number of religious societies whose members made only simple vows. Even when, as happened in a few cases, these congregations possessed the privilege of exemption, they were not considered to be regulars. This is clear from a response of the Sacred Congregation of Bishops and Regulars.[42] Consequently they were not bound by the laws enacted for regulars. As a matter of fact there was no common law for these congregations before the

[37] Piat, *Praelectiones*, I, 657-658.

[38] Urban VIII, decr., "*Sacra,*" 21 sept. 1624, § 6—*Bull. Rom. Taur.*, XIII, 205.

[39] Clement VIII, const., "*Nullus omnino,*" 25 iul. 1599, § 6—*Bull. Rom. Taur.*, X, 664.

[40] *Praelectiones*, I, 657.

[41] *Op. cit.*, 659.

[42] *Congregationis Presbyterorum Saecularium*, 16 sept. 1864—*Fontes*, n. 1993.

Constitution of Leo XIII *"Conditae a Christo,"* which determined the relation between these societies and the local ordinary. As a result, these congregations were governed entirely by their own constitutions, which, when they were approved by the Holy See, constituted particular law for them. There was at most a common practice which the Sacred Congregation of Bishops and Regulars was accustomed to follow in approving these societies and in solving difficulties submitted by them. This practice was formulated in the *Normae* published by this Sacred Congregation in 1901.[43] In order to give a general idea of the chapter as it existed among these congregations, it is here described as outlined in these *Normae,* together with references to some of the pre-Code authors. It should be kept in mind that the *Normae* did not constitute law, but were merely the norms which the Sacred Congregation followed in approving these congregations.

The *Normae* do not make any provision for a local chapter. They do, however, reserve to the local community the right to choose a delegate to the provincial chapter if the congregation is divided into provinces, or to the general chapter if it has not been so divided.[44] The decree of the Sacred Congregation of Religious already mentioned, which prescribed that everyone in a community of women religious had the right to vote on retaining the ordinary confessor, applied also to congregations of women of simple vows.[45]

The provincial chapter, where it was required by the constitutions, was composed of the provincial superior and his council, local superiors of houses having at least twelve members, and a delegate from each house chosen by the members of the community.[46] Whatever powers it had, it had from the particular constitutions of the institute. According to the *Normae,* it chose two delegates, and substitutes for these, to the general chapter.[47]

[43] *Normae secundum quas Sacra Congregatio Episcoporum et Regularium in novis religiosis congregationibus approbandis procedere solet* (Romae, 1901).

[44] *Normae,* art. 216, 221; Vermeersch, *De Religiosis,* II, n. 104.

[45] 3 febr. 1913, n. 2, (b)—*Fontes,* n. 4416.

[46] *Normae,* art. 221; Vermeersch, *De Religiosis,* II, n. 114.

[47] Art. 220-221.

Every congregation had a general chapter.[48] It was either ordinary, which met every six or twelve years according to the constitutions; or extraordinary, which was convened at intermediate intervals, as, for example, if the death of the Superior General made an election necessary. If these intermediate chapters were called for any other reason than the death of the Superior General, a majority vote of the general council and the permission of the Holy See was required.[49]

The chapter was convoked by letter of the Superior General, or his vicar, three months before the chapter if the congregation was confined to Europe, and six months before the time of the chapter if the congregation had extended beyond Europe.[50] It was to be convened at the place decided upon by the Superior General with the deliberative vote of his council.[51]

The composition of the chapter differed as the congregation was divided into provinces or not. In either case the Superior General, his councillors, the secretary general and the general econome, had the right of suffrage in the general chapter. The constitutions could permit that former Superiors General would also have the right of suffrage in chapter.[52] If the congregation was divided into provinces, the provincial superior with the delegates chosen by the provincial chapter completed the general chapter.[53] If the congregation was not divided into provinces the chapter was completed by the local superiors and delegates chosen by the local communities. Not all houses, however, could send these representatives. The superiors of only those houses that had twelve or more members had the right of suffrage in the general chapter. These same communities could also elect a delegate. Provision was to be made for the smaller houses to

[48] Vermeersch, *De Religiosis,* I, n. 408.

[49] *Normae,* art. 206, 207, 210; Vermeersch, *De Religiosis,* II, n. 107; Battandier, *Guide Canonique pour les Constitutions des Instituts à Voeux Simples* (3. ed., Paris, 1905), nn. 291, 293 (hereafter cited as Battandier, *Guide Canonique*).

[50] *Normae,* art. 211; Vermeersch, *De Religiosis,* II, n. 107; Battandier, *Guide Canonique,* n. 294.

[51] *Normae,* art. 212.

[52] *Normae,* art. 213-214.

[53] *Normae,* art. 220-222.

unite in order to reach the number of twelve members and then choose one superior and one delegate. If this unity of action was impossible because of distance, then a smaller community could unite with a larger one and have equal right in electing the delegate.[54] It was required for validity that two-thirds of those having the right of suffrage should be present at the general chapter.[55]

The chapter was presided over by the Superior General, or his vicar. In chapters when a new superior was elected, the superior elected presided after the election.[56] In congregations of women the local ordinary presided until the elections were completed; then the superioress presided.[57]

The general chapter exercised the supreme power in the congregation.[58] Principally it was concerned with elections, and elected the Superior General, the general councillors, the secretary general, and the general econome.[59] Other matters of grave importance pertaining to the general chapter were those especially which could not be transacted without the permission of the Holy See.[60] An example of this was a change in constitutions which had been approved by the Holy See.[61]

[54] *Normae,* art. 215, 219.

[55] *Normae,* art. 223.

[56] *Normae,* art. 225, 227.

[57] Leo XIII, const., *"Conditae a Christo,"* 8 dec. 1900, § 2, I—*Fontes,* n 644; *Normae,* art. 224.

[58] *Normae,* art. 203.

[59] *Normae,* art. 231, 239.

[60] *Normae,* art. 246.

[61] Battandier, *Guide Canonique,* n. 337.

HISTORICAL CONCLUSION

This brief study of the historical development of chapters as conducted among religious shows that in great part they were governed by the particular laws proper to each institute. This is in accord with the constant policy of the Church in regard to legislation for the internal government of religious societies. The Church has never attempted to form them in one mold by a common legislation equally binding upon all in every particular; but having approved their constitutions, the Church set these up as the law by which they were to be guided. To do otherwise would not have been in keeping with the diversity of aims and purposes which the various founders had in establishing their societies and which the Church herself endorsed by her approbation. When it was necessary to enact some common legislation, exception was frequently made for contrary prescriptions of particular constitutions and privileges. This same practice is very evident in the present legislation for religious in the Code of Canon Law, for with striking regularity there occur such phrases as, *ad normam constitutionum, secundum constitutiones, nisi aliud constitutiones caveant, si ita ferant constitutiones,* and the like. Still from the historical study of these chapters some general conclusions concerning their development can be drawn.

The local chapter seems to have originated with the Rule of St. Benedict. Beginning with a merely consultative voice, the community gradually developed into a deliberative body possessing decisive rights in certain matters. In some cases ecclesiastical law added a sanction invalidating the action of the superior if he failed to obtain the consent of the chapter when it was required. Always, however, saving the case where the right of election belonged to the local chapter and then only as to the election was its competence positive, its power was negative, consisting in a right to prevent the superior from acting. It could not force him to act.

The next chapter to appear in order of time was the general chapter, that is, one representative of the whole order. This came with the founding of the Cistercians.

Following this and under the influence of the popes, particularly of Innocent III, there arose the provincial chapter, a regional chapter based upon the boundaries of some province or kingdom. Its purpose was to provide whatever was necessary for the reform of the monastic life and the promotion of the regular observance. Ecclesiastical law gave it the right to legislate for this purpose and a means to enforce its enactments in its right to appoint visitors. Both this and the general chapter were what might be called aristocratic in that they were composed entirely of abbots or conventual priors, that is, of superiors. A change in the provincial chapter was introduced by the Mendicant orders. As it existed among them it was not regulated by the boundaries of an already existing province or kingdom, but the religious society itself was divided into provinces. With the rise of the Mendicant orders, there arose also the representative system in chapters. Besides the superiors, who were themselves chosen in chapter by the members of the institute, the chapter embraced delegates elected by the religious.

The convocation of the chapter, the right to preside in the chapter and the right of suffrage in chapter were regulated by the particular laws of each institute. The right of suffrage, especially in regard to chapters of election, was subject to the restrictive prescriptions of common law.

The powers of the chapter were in great part founded upon common law, but were usually modified by the particular constitutions and privileges of each institute.

Since there was, practically speaking, no common law for the congregations of simple vows before the promulgation of the Code of Canon Law, the chapters in these institutes were governed almost entirely by their own constitutions. There were, however, certain requirements, constituting what might be called a common practice, demanded by the norms which the Sacred Congregation followed in giving approbation to these constitutions.

Part II

Canonical Commentary

CHAPTER V

THE AUTHORITY OF RELIGIOUS CHAPTERS

Canon 501: § 1. . . . Capitula, ad normam constitutionum et iuris communis, potestatem habent dominativam in subditos; in religione autem clericali exempta, habent iurisdictionem ecclesiasticam tam pro foro interno, quam pro externo.

§ 2. Superioribus quibuslibet districte prohibetur quominus in causis ad S. Officium spectantibus se intromittant.

The scope of the present chapter is to investigate the extent of the authority possessed by religious chapters. The foundation, or the guiding principle for such an investigation is laid down in canon 501, cited above, where it is declared that all chapters have dominative power and that the chapters in clerical exempt institutes have ecclesiastical jurisdiction, according to the norms of the constitutions and common law. Since any attempt to investigate the constitutions of particular religious institutes would be an endless task, the present study will be based principally upon the prescriptions of common law. Before attempting to determine the extent of these powers, it will not be out of place to premise a few remarks on their nature.

Article 1. The Nature of the Authority

A. *As to Dominative Power*

1. Concept. Etymologically, dominative power is the authority which a master had over his slaves. With the disappearance of slavery

there arose a new relationship based on a free agreement between master and servant. This was called herile society and here also the authority of the master was called dominative or domestic power and extended to all matters covered by the free agreement. By extension the term was used to designate the authority exercised in any imperfect society.[1] The peculiar dominative power mentioned in canon 501 is that to which religious, both men and women, become subject by reason of their free entrance into the society of some religious institute. The Code of Canon Law never explicitly treats of the nature of this dominative power, not defining it even in a general way as it does in regard to ecclesiastical jurisdiction.[2] The practically unanimous opinion of authors,[3] both before and after the promulgation of the Code, is that dominative power is a *private* power.[4] It is usually

[1] Blat, "De Potestate Superiorum in Religionibus secundum Codicem I. C."—*CpRM,* XVI (1935), 324. Cf. also Vermeersch, *De Religiosis,* I, n. 388.

[2] Canon 196: "Potestas iurisdictionis seu *regiminis.* . . ."

[3] This power is designated in various ways by authors; e. g., social, domestic, economic, etc.; but, as Pejška justly remarks, this multiplication of terms offers no particular advantage to the study of this subject and is merely burdensome. Cf. *Ius Canonicum Religiosorum* (3. ed., Friburgi Brisgoviae: Herder, 1927), p. 119 (hereafter cited as Pejška, *Ius Canonicum Religiosorum*). Following the Code of Canon Law this study will use the term *dominative.*

[4] E. g., Vermeersch, *De Religiosis,* I, nn. 388, 402; Vermeersch-Creusen, *Epitome Iuris Canonici Cum Commentariis ad Scholas et Usum Privatorum* (3 vols., Romae: H. Dessain, Vol. I, 1937), I, n. 619 (hereafter cited as Vermeersch-Creusen, *Epitome*); Piat, *Praelectiones,* I, pp. 598-599; Blat, "De Potestate Superiorum in Religionibus secundum Codicem I. C."—*CpRM,* XVI (1935), 325; Schaefer, *De Religiosis,* p. 221; Pejška, *Ius Canonicum Religiosorum,* p. 229. On the contrary, Coronata (*Institutiones,* I, n. 527) calls it *formaliter* public. Larraona ("De Potestate Dominativa Publica in Iure Canonico"—*Acta Congressus Iuridici Internationalis* [5 vols., Romae: Apud Custodiam Librariam Pont. Instituti Utriusque Iuris, Vol. IV, 1937], 148) while admitting that, before the promulgation of the Code, dominative power was considered to be private in every respect, thinks it would be worthwhile to investigate the status of this power in pre-Code law and see if this were really true. He positively denies that, under the present legislation, the dominative power in religious institutes is merely a private power: "Non vacat nunc investigare an haec divisio doctrinalis potestatis, quae adaequata atque simplex videbatur dum publica a privatis separabat, vero iuris statui ante Codicem responderet necne; post ipsum, nisi multum fallimur, absolute non respondet. . . . Sed pariter satis

described as the right acquired by a religious institute to govern the religious society and direct it toward the attaining of both the common end of the religious state and the proper end of the society, according to the norms of the constitutions and the common law.[5]

2. Source. The proximate source from which religious chapters draw their dominative power is the constitutions, that is, the particular laws which determine the hierarchy of government in the institute. The remote source, that from which this power ultimately arises, cannot be definitely designated. The sources given by authors are the private wills of those forming the religious society,[6] the vow of obedience,[7] the quasi-contract of religious profession,[8] and the natural law conferring on every society legitimately established the authority necessary for its direction and conservation.[9] The best opinion seems to be the one which holds that the source from which this authority arises is the hypothetical natural law which confers on every society legitimately established the authority necessary to conserve and govern it. It is by the religious profession, as by quasi-contract, that this authority is extended to individual religious. It could hardly arise from the vow of obedience since it extends to

clarum videtur, in Codice admissam seu ex Codice ac necessario admittendam esse potestatem, quae, etsi non possit confundi cum stricta potestate iurisdictionis, . . . ad potestatem iurisdictionis ita accedit ut, in illis quae juris positive sunt, ipsius characterem publicum certo et clare participet." He supports this view with good arguments, but this is an academic question and further consideration of it would be of no particular advantage to this study.

[5] E.g., Chelodi, *Ius de Personis,* n. 252; Pejška, *Ius Canonicum Religiosorum,* p. 158; Berutti, *De Religiosis,* n. 25; Wernz-Vidal, *Ius Canonicum,* III, n. 93; Coronata, *Institutiones,* I, n. 527; Piat, *Praelectiones,* I, p. 598; Schaefer, *De Religiosis,* p. 221; Vermeersch, *De Religiosis,* I, n. 401; Augustine, *A Commentary on the New Code of Canon Law* (8 vols., St. Louis, Mo.: Herder, Vol. II, 6. ed., 1936; Vol. III, 5. ed., 1938), III, p. 104 (hereafter cited as Augustine, *A Commentary*); Blat, "De Potestate Superiorum in Religionibus secundum Codicem I. C."—*CpRM,* XVI (1935), 325.

[6] Blat, *loc. cit.*; Fanfani, *De Iure Religiosorum,* n. 51.

[7] Berutti, *De Religiosis,* n. 23.

[8] Coronata, *Institutiones,* I, n. 527; Pejška, *Ius Canonicum Religiosorum,* p. 138.

[9] Cappello, *Summa Iuris Canonici,* II, n. 567; Wernz-Vidal, *Ius Canonicum,* III, n. 93; Vermeersch, *De Religiosis,* I, n. 402; Schaefer, *De Religiosis,* p. 221; Augustine, *A Commentary,* III, p. 104.

many things in no way touched by the vow of obedience, e. g., administration of the temporal goods, admission of new members, etc. The vow of obedience is rather a powerful, and extraordinary, means of enforcing this authority, imposing, as it does, a specific obligation from the virtue of religion when the superior legitimately commands by virtue of the vow.[10]

B. *As to Ecclesiastical Jurisdiction*

1. Concept. Canon 196 explains in a general way the nature of ecclesiastical jurisdiction when it describes it as the power of ruling which the Church has from its divine institution. This is the public power with which every perfect society is endowed. It is defined as: The public power of a legitimate superior, conceded by Christ, or by the Church through canonical mission, of ruling the baptized in relation to eternal salvation.[11] This power of ruling embraces all the powers by which the faithful can in any way be directed toward this end and, therefore, it contains legislative, judicial, coercive and executive or administrative authority. The objects of this authority, directly, are spiritual things or things necessarily connected with spiritual things; indirectly, it extends also to temporal things.[12] According to the different effects which the exercise of this power has, that is, whether it obliges before the Church or before God only, it is called jurisdiction of the internal or external forum.[13] When the jurisdiction

[10] Pejška, *Ius Canonicum Religiosorum,* 139-140; Van Hove, *De Legibus Ecclesiasticis—Commentarium Lovaniense in Codicem Iuris Canonici, editum a Magistris et Doctoribus Universitatis Lovaniensis* (Romae: H. Dessain, Vol. I, Tom. II, 1930), n. 357 (hereafter cited as Van Hove, *De Legibus*).

[11] Maroto, *Institutiones Iuris Canonici ad Normam Novi Codicis* (2 vols., Matriti: Editorial del corazon de Maria, Vol. I, 1919), I, n. 573 (hereafter cited as Maroto, *Institutiones*).

[12] Maroto, *loc. cit.*

[13] Blat, "De Potestate Superiorum in Religionibus secundum Codicem I. C."—*CpRM,* XVI (1935), 329. Others explain this distinction as to forum somewhat differently; they say that jurisdiction of the external forum is that which is exercised primarily for the good of the society and affects the individual only insofar as he is a member of the society, while jurisdiction of the internal forum is that which is exercised for the good of the individual as such. Cf. Maroto, *Institutiones,* I, n. 573.

is attached to an office by the law it is called *ordinary,* which may be either proper or vicarious; when it is committed to a person it is called *delegated.*[14]

The concession of jurisdiction to chapters by canon 501 is a general concession and so must be understood without restrictions; hence, in clerical exempt institutes, according to common law, all chapters have ecclesiastical jurisdiction.[15] This jurisdiction is, moreover, ordinary and proper.[16]

2. Source. Ultimately the jurisdiction of the religious chapter is derived from the Divine Founder of the Church, Jesus Christ; proximately it is conferred on it in the same way it is conferred on all superiors subordinate to the Roman Pontiff, by canonical mission.[17] This canonical mission by which jurisdiction is conferred in respect to religious chapters is found in the legitimate assembling of a chapter, which, according to common and particular law, is endowed with it.[18]

Article II. The Extent of the Authority

When considering the extent of the authority of religious chapters, one must take particular note of the restriction placed on the authority of any religious superior whatsoever, and, consequently, of chapters, which are in reality collegiate superiors, by canon 501, § 2. This section of canon 501 strictly forbids any interference by religious superiors in causes which pertain to the competence of the Holy Office. These causes are all which pertain to the doctrine of faith and morals,[19] some of the most grave abuses of the sacraments especially

[14] Canon 197.

[15] Coronata, *Institutiones,* I, n. 534 (and p. 646, note 6); Schaefer, *De Religiosis,* p. 232.

[16] Larraona, "Commentarium Codicis"—*CpR,* VII (1926), 35.

[17] Canon 109.

[18] Blat, "De Potestate Superiorum in Religionibus secundum Codicem I. C."—*CpRM,* XVI (1935), 330.

[19] Canon 247. Hence the crimes of heresy, apostasy from the faith, schism (canon 2314, § 2); other crimes which render one juridically suspect of heresy (canons 2316; 2319, § 2; 2320; 2332; 2340, § 1; 2371); or are connected with heresy (canons 2317, 2318). Cf. Schaefer, *De Religiosis,* p. 223; Larraona, "Commentarium Codicis"—*CpR,* VII (1926), 93-94.

when proceeding from a false doctrine,[20] cases attacking the validity of ordination because of a substantial defect of the sacred rite,[21] and finally cases touching the Eucharistic fast for priests celebrating Mass.[22] A decree of the Holy Office itself of May 15, 1901, cited by Cardinal Gasparri as one of the sources of this law,[23] clearly explains what is forbidden to superiors. It says that in these matters religious superiors cannot and should not, under any title or pretext, make inquiries, receive accusations, question witnesses, punish the guilty, institute judgment, pass sentence, or in any other form or fashion concern themselves with them or take them up. For our purpose here it may be simply stated that these causes are altogether outside the competence of any religious chapter.[24]

The only decisive norm for determining the actual extent of the authority of any religious chapter or for determining whether some act is within the competence of a particular chapter, is the particular law of the religious institute, for in not one place in the canons is any particular act definitely and positively committed to any particular chapter.[25] Since this is so, there is no particular advantage

[20] Viz.: solicitation (canons 904, 2368); the violation of the seal (canons 889, 890, 2369); the qualified inquiry of the name of an accomplice (canon 888, § 2; cf., however, Larraona, "Commentarium Codicis"—*CpR*, VII [1926], 95); and the celebration of Mass and the administration of the sacrament of penance without the order of priesthood (canon 2322, 1°). Cf. Schaefer and Larraona, *loc. cit.*

[21] Canon 1993.

[22] Canon 247. There are other cases concerning marriage which are exclusively within the competence of the Holy Office which need not be mentioned when treating of the jurisdiction in religious institutes (cf. canons 247, § 3; 1962).

[23] S. C. S. Off., decr. 15 maii 1901—*Fontes*, n. 1254.

[24] Because of this prohibition of canon 501, § 2, Larraona says that crimes within the competence of the Holy Office cannot be material for canonical warning or cause for dismissal. It would not however be forbidden to religious superiors to take action which would in no way pertain to or interfere with the juridic handling of these causes; e. g., to transfer a religious, to remove him from danger of relapse by preventing him from hearing confessions, etc.—"Commentarium Codicis"—*CpR*, VII (1926), 96 (and note 182). Cf. also Schaefer, *De Religiosis*, p. 224.

[25] There are some places where particular acts of administration are committed to religious chapters, but it is in the provisory way, unless the consti-

to be gained by considering the three types of religious chapters—general, provincial and local—and trying to determine their authority. It seems much more satisfactory to take up the various species of authority and attempt to determine to what extent they are within the competence of religious chapters generally considered. Particular applications will have to be made by consulting the particular laws of individual religious institutes.

A. *Legislative Authority*

The jurisdiction conferred on chapters in clerical exempt institutes includes also legislative power so that they can enact laws, strictly so-called, for the whole religious institute or for some part of it.[26] It is not true to say that only the general chapter in these societies can pass laws,[27] for from the nature of the jurisdiction all chapters in these societies have legislative power and some provincial chapters actually exercise it.[28] It is only from the particular laws of the institute that one can determine which chapters can make laws.

No religious chapter can enact laws contrary to common law or to the Rules and Constitutions of the institute since these derive their authority from a power superior to the chapter, nor can any chapter authentically interpret the Rules and Constitutions unless this authority has been given to it.[29] A chapter can, however, authen-

tutions provide otherwise (e. g., canon 494, § 2); or disjunctively, either to the chapter or superior (canons 563; 587, § 1; 597, § 3); or to the superior with council or chapter (canons 534, § 1; 543; 646, § 2; 655, § 1; 667). A possible exception to this is the case of deciding on the retention of the ordinary confessor (canon 526); but this does not seem to be a capitular action strictly so-called, for all members of the community, not only chapter members, have the right of suffrage, and this question must be decided in this way even if in some particular institute a local or conventual chapter is not had.

[26] Schaefer, *De Religiosis,* p. 233; Coronata, *Institutiones,* I, n. 534, 3° and p. 651, note 2.

[27] E. g., Berutti, *De Religiosis,* n. 24: ". . . leges vero condi nequeunt nisi in Capitulis generalibus Religionum clericalium exemptarum. . . ."

[28] E. g., among the Passionists. Cf. Aloisius a S. Francisco Paulano, *De Capitulis Habendis in Congregatione Clericorum Excalceatorum SS. Crucis et Passionis D. N. J. C.* (Romae: ex Typographia Pontificia in Instituto Pii X, 1920), p. 96 (hereafter cited as Aloisius a S. Francisco Paulano, *De Capitulis*).

[29] Canon 17.

tically interpret and even abrogate the laws of chapters which preceded it since it is the same legislative authority which acts in both cases.[80]

The chapters in non-exempt religious institutes, since they lack jurisdiction, cannot pass laws, strictly so-called. They can, however, enact regulations binding upon those subject to their authority. Whatever these may be called—regulations, capitular constitutions, statutes, etc.—they are in reality general precepts based upon dominative power. They cannot establish anything contrary to common law, or to the Rules and Constitutions approved by pontifical or episcopal authority. It is commonly taught that these enactments are not perpetual but endure only until the succeeding chapter.[81] Maroto, however, defends the enduring nature of such precepts.[82] No support for either opinion can be drawn from the Code since nowhere does it legislate for general precepts.[83] The common opinion that they endure only until the succeeding chapter is probably based on the *Normae* of 1901,[84] but, as everyone knows, these are not law. They do, however, give an indication of what is ordinarily true in regard to these congregations of simple vows inasmuch as they are the norms which the Holy See followed in approving such congregations. It can safely be presumed then that these precepts endure only until the succeeding chapter. This presumption must, however, give way to fact if the particular laws of some institute determine that capitular constitutions are perpetual. If they are found to be perpetual a succeeding chapter can authentically interpret or abrogate them.[85]

80 Canons 17, 22. If these laws were approved by the Holy See *in forma specifica* they would be pontifical laws and hence beyond the competence of succeeding chapters.

81 Van Hove, *De Legibus*, n. 359 and p. 363, note 2; Schaefer, *De Religiosis*, pp. 232-233; Coronata, *Institutiones*, I, n. 534.

82 *Institutiones*, I, n. 268.

83 It is doubtful if canon 24 which determines the nature of precepts given to individuals applies to precepts coming from dominative power. Cf. Van Hove, *De Legibus*, n. 356.

84 Art. 250.

85 If approved by pontifical or episcopal authority *in forma specifica* they would be perpetual and could be changed or authentically interpreted only by permission of the authority confirming them.

The nature of the obligation arising from these capitular laws or precepts is determined by the title under which they are imposed; hence, violation of a precept based on dominative power is an offense only against obedience, while violation of a law or precept based on jurisdiction is an offense also against the virtue toward which the law or precept is directed, at least if the authority imposing it wished to regard the thing commanded as pertaining to the subject matter of this virtue.[86] Whether these laws or precepts oblige under pain of sin or only under the penalty imposed for violation depends on the will of the authority imposing them. However, even if the Rules and Constitutions do not oblige under pain of sin, from the very nature of jurisdiction and dominative power, these laws and precepts can impose an obligation binding in conscience under pain of sin, either mortal or venial, depending upon the gravity of the matter and the intention of the authority imposing them.[87]

B. Elective Authority

Perhaps the most important authority of religious chapters at the present time is their power to designate by election superiors for the ordinary government of the institute. The extent of this authority can be learned solely from the particular law of the individual religious societies, for the canons confer no electoral right upon any chapter. It is true, indeed, that they recognize that some religious superiors are elected in chapter and legislate for the method of conducting these elections,[88] but nowhere do they expressly prescribe that the appointment of any superior must be made by capitular election.

Closely allied with the elective authority of chapters is the right

[86] Cf. Van Hove, *De Legibus*, n. 360; Arregui, *Summarium Theologiae Moralis ad Recentem Codicem Iuris Canonici Accommodatum* (12. ed., Bilbao: El mensajero del Corazon de Jesus, 1934), n. 52 (hereafter cited as Arregui, *Summarium*).

[87] Schaefer, *De Religiosis*, p. 233; Goyeneche, "Consultationes"—*CpR*, V (1924), 281-282.

[88] Major superiors in institutes of men religious, the superioress in a monastery of nuns and the Supreme Moderator in a Congregation of women religious. Cf. canons 506-507. The method of conducting capitular elections will be treated in a later chapter.

of postulation, the act which proposes to the competent superior the choice of a candidate who is able and worthy to fill an office, but is excluded by the requirement of some law from which the superior can dispense and usually does not refuse to grant the dispensation.[39] The Church, as is clear from the prescription of canon 507, § 3, is opposed to postulation in religious chapters and permits it in extraordinary cases only and as long as it is not forbidden by the Constitutions.[40]

In connection with the elective authority it may be asked whether it is within the competence of a chapter which has elected a superior to accept his renunciation. A distinction must be made in answering this question. If there is question of the renunciation of an election, certainly it is within the competence of a chapter to accept the renunciation and proceed to a new election.[41] If, however, it is the renunciation of an office which had once been accepted, it depends on whether or not the election needed confirmation. If the election were confirmed then only the superior who confirmed the election could accept the renunciation.[42] If the election did not need confirmation then the chapter, since it completely conferred the office, could accept the renunciation.[43]

C. Administrative Authority

The administrative or executive power of chapters receives but little attention in the canons, and so, for the most part must be discovered from the particular laws of the institute. Authors make the general statement that chapters have greater power than superiors and therefore to them are reserved the more weighty affairs of the institute.[44] The actual determination of these will have to be made by

[39] Canon 179.

[40] "Postulatio admitti potest solum in casu extraordinario et dummodo in constitutionibus non prohibeatur."

[41] Cf. canons 175-176.

[42] Cf. canon 187, § 2.

[43] Canon 187, § 1; cf. Pejška, *Ius Canonicum Religiosorum,* p. 218.

[44] E. g., Coronata, *Institutiones,* I, n. 535. For example, they would reserve to the general chapter the right to decide whether a change in the constitutions were necessary. This is also the mind of the Sacred Congregation for Religious,

the particular law. It is desirable, however, to consider some prescriptions of the canons. Unless the constitutions decree otherwise, it belongs to the general chapter, during the time of chapter, to decide about the disposition of the goods of a province that has ceased to exist.[45] Disjunctively with the superior, the general chapter has the right to approve houses for study in clerical institutes [46] and to determine and change the limits of the cloister in institutes of men of solemn vows.[47] There are other places in the Code where the canons prescribe that the superior, in order to act, must have either the advice or consent of either his council or the chapter: to proceed with alienation and the contracting of debts; [48] to admit aspirants to the novitiate or religious profession; [49] to issue a declaration of ipso facto dismissal; [50] and to confer the faculty of dismissing in distant places to some good and prudent religious.[51] The determination of whether this right belongs to the council or the chapter will depend upon the constitutions of each institute.

D. Dispensing Authority

1. From general ecclesiastical laws. The Code nowhere commits to religious chapters any power to dispense from general ecclesiastical laws. Therefore, they have no power in this matter.[52]

for in a declaration of October 26, 1921, it is stated: "Such a petition will not be accepted, however, by this Sacred Congregation, unless the proposed changes have been discussed and approved by the General Chapter."—*Acta Apostolicae Sedis, Commentarium Officiale* (Romae, 1909—), XIII, 538 (hereafter cited as *AAS*). Translation from Bouscaren, *Canon Law Digest* (2 vols. and Supplement, Milwaukee: Bruce, 1934, 1937, Suppl., 1941), I, 272 (hereafter cited as Bouscaren, *Canon Law Digest*).

[45] Canon 494, § 2.

[46] Canon 587, § 1.

[47] Canon 597, § 3.

[48] Canon 534, § 1.

[49] Canon 543. This suffrage for the first profession is deliberative, for perpetual profession it is consultative (canon 575, § 2). The nature of the suffrage for admission to the novitiate is not determined in common law.

[50] Canon 646, § 2.

[51] Canon 667.

[52] Cf. canons 80-81. Even if chapters have ordinary jurisdiction they are not Ordinaries in the canonical sense. Cf. canon 198.

2. From the Rules and Constitutions. The only faculty of dispensing from the Rules and Constitutions conceded to religious superiors by the common law is to dispense from some acts of the community for reasons of study.[53] There seems to be no reason to exclude religious chapters from the use of this faculty, since they are truly superiors. Whatever other faculties chapters possess in this matter can be discovered only by investigating the particular laws of the institute.

3. From capitular laws and statutes. Unless such capitular enactments, by reason of approval, have become pontifical or episcopal laws, chapters can dispense in their own laws or precepts and in those of their predecessors.[54]

E. Judicial Authority

In institutes in which the superiors and chapters do not have ecclesiastical jurisdiction there is no judicial authority strictly so-called. Whoever acts by reason of dominative power only can use only a paternal or administrative process. Whether and to what extent chapters in these institutes possess such authority can be determined only from the particular constitutions.

The Code in setting up tribunals for clerical exempt institutes makes no mention of chapters as enjoying judicial power, but only of provincial superiors, local abbots, and Supreme Moderators of institutes or monastic congregations.[55] Concerning the tribunal of first instance, however, provision is made in canon 1579, § 1 for diverse prescriptions of the constitutions. These constitutions could, then, give judicial power to chapters; but if they do not, the chapters have no judicial authority and cannot institute any judicial process.[56]

[53] Canon 589, § 2.

[54] Canon 80; cf. Pejška, *Ius Canonicum Religiosorum*, p. 219. Chapters with dominative power only have the power of dispensing not in the strict but only in a broad sense. In the *Normae* of 1901 (art. 265) it is called "auctoritas eximendi."

[55] Canons 1579, §§ 1-2; 1594, § 4.

[56] Cf. Pejška, *Ius Canonicum Religiosorum*, p. 219.

F. Coercive and Punitive Authority

Chapters having dominative power only cannot inflict any canonical penalty strictly so-called. They can, however, add to their precepts penal remedies or penances for violation. The restrictions on this authority can be learned only from the particular law of the institute.[57]

Chapters in clerical exempt institutes by reason of jurisdiction have strict coercive power and can inflict all canonical penalties.[58] To what extent particular chapters can exercise this power can be learned only from the particular laws of each institute. Chapters in these institutes, however, cannot reserve sins since the Code restricts the right to do this to the Superior General in clerical exempt institutes and to the abbot of a monastery *sui iuris*.[59]

In regard to the punitive authority of a religious chapter it may be asked if it is within its competence to deprive of his office a superior whom it has legitimately elected. Among the authors who wrote on the law for regulars before the promulgation of the Code it seems to have been the generally accepted opinion that superiors elected in chapter could be deposed by the same chapter. Piat and Vermeersch may be cited as representative of this opinion. Piat in treating of the power of the general chapter says that it can elect, punish and even depose the superior general, since it is so provided in the constitutions of all orders;[60] in his treatment of the authority of the provincial chapter, he says that it can elect the provincial superior, other superiors and local prelates and, *de iure communi*, can depose them. He bases this statement on the rule of law: *Omnis res, per quascumque causas nascitur, per easdem dissolvitur*.[61]

[57] Cf. Coronata, *Institutiones*, I, n. 534; Schaefer, *De Religiosis*, pp. 228-229.

[58] Berutti, *De Religiosis*, nn. 24, 26; Schaefer, *De Religiosis*, p. 228; Coronata, *Institutiones*, I, n. 534.

[59] Canon 896.

[60] *Praelectiones*, I, p. 659. In a footnote to this statement he cites Pellizzarius, Antonius a Sp. Sancto, Rotarius, Suarez, Donatus, de Lezana and de Peyrinis.

[61] *Praelectiones*, I, p. 660. The rule of law quoted is taken from the Decretals of Gregory IX (c. 1, X, *de regulis iuris*, V, 41). Cited in a footnote to this statement are Pellizzarius, de Lezana and Antonius a Sp. Sancto.

Vermeersch says substantially the same in regard to both general and provincial chapter, but gives no reasons and cites no authorities.[62]

Among the authors who wrote after the promulgation of the Code, Augustine repeats in substance the teaching of Piat and Vermeersch.[63] The writer has been able to find no other author who treats the question in a general way. Some authors do consider the particular question whether the general chapter can depose the Superior General, but they differ in their solutions. Wernz-Vidal and Coronata say the general chapter can depose the Superior General, unless it is otherwise established by particular law.[64] Schaefer, on the contrary, says that the extent of the punitive authority of the general chapter over the Supreme Superior must be drawn from the particular law, but that his deposal must be considered a major cause and is, therefore, reserved to the Roman Pontiff.[65] None of the four modern authors here considered cites any sources or proposes any reasons to support his opinion.

Pejška[66] treats the question more fully. After asking the question whether the chapter can depose the Supreme Moderator he answers definitely in the negative. His reasons are: (1) The convocation of a general chapter, before the office is actually vacant, to depose the Superior General and consequently to elect another is of no juridic effect by reason of canon 162, § 5. (2) If it is an irremovable office, a superior can be deprived of it only through process of law (canon 192, § 2) before a tribunal of three judges (canon 1576, § 1, 1°). (3) Because of canon 195 a general chapter that has elected a Superior General cannot deprive him of office. At length, however, he tones down his original categorical negative by saying that a chapter could more readily remove a Superior General elected

[62] *De Religiosis*, I, nn. 404-405.

[63] *A Commentary*, III, p. 108.

[64] Wernz-Vidal, *Ius Canonicum*, III, n. 107; Coronata, *Institutiones*, I, n. 535. Coronata seems to depend on Piat, at least the similarity of expression is striking; Piat: "Generalem eligere, punire, imo et deponere potest. . . ." Coronata: ". . . eligit Superiorem supremum eumque corrigere et punire, immo et deponere potest. . . ."

[65] *De Religiosis*, p. 232.

[66] *Ius Canonicum Religiosorum*, p. 219.

for a definite term of years, if during that time he proved incapable, unless he had been confirmed by the Holy See or the Bishop.

To sum up, the state of the question is this. Authors who treat of the law of regulars before the Code seem to have held that chapters which elected a superior could also deprive him of office. Writing after the Code: Augustine follows the opinion of pre-Code writers; Wernz-Vidal and Coronata say the general chapter can deprive the Superior General of his office; Pejška denies this, except in the case of a temporary Superior General not confirmed by the Holy See or the Bishop; Schaefer considers the deposal of the Supreme Superior a major cause reserved to the Holy See. How is the question to be solved? In the solution which follows it must be kept in mind that the question to be settled is what the religious chapter can do in this matter under the common law; for, as everyone knows, particular law passed by competent authority can derogate from the general law. Hence, if by valid particular law any chapter has such power it cannot be doubted that it can exercise it.

The common law as contained in the canons has no special prescriptions concerning the privation of office in religious institutes and it does not specifically impose on these religious societies the general laws for privation of office as it does the general laws for elections.[67] However, there can be no question that these general laws do apply when there is question of an ecclesiastical office in the strict sense, since there is no reason to exclude such offices from their application. Therefore, because of the clear prescription of canon 195,[68] any chapter which has elected a cleric to an office, strictly so-called, cannot deprive him of that office. From the prescription of canon 501, § 1, superiors in clerical exempt institutes have ecclesiastical jurisdiction and hence have an ecclesiastical office in the strict sense so that the chapter which elected them cannot deprive them of office. Larraona leans toward the opinion that even in clerical non-exempt institutes the superiors have an ecclesiastical office in the

[67] Cf. canon 507.

[68] "Qui clericum ad officium elegerunt vel postulaverunt aut praesentaverunt, nequeunt eundem officio privare aut ab eo revocare seu amovere aut ad aliud transferre."

strict sense.[69] If this be true, then in these institutes also the chapter which elected a superior cannot deprive him of his office.

Can this prescription of canon 195 apply also to religious offices which are not such in the strict sense? It does not seem that, under a literal interpretation, canon 195 can be so extended, for in the law the word *"officium"* is to be understood in the strict sense unless the contrary appears from the context.[70] Since, then, there is lacking in this matter a definite prescription of law, is it permissible to apply this canon by way of analogy, according to the norm of canon 20? It seems that it would be, for it is not a question here of applying a penalty but of restricting the right to inflict a penalty.[71] Moreover, this is a law passed not only for a like matter but for the very same matter and the only distinction present is based on the nature of the offices involved. Since these chapters are obliged to abide by the general laws for elections, it seems that they should also be obliged by the consequences of election established in the same laws. Hence it seems that, by reason of canon 195, religious chapters cannot deprive a superior, whom they have legitimately elected, of his office even if it be an office only in the broad sense.

[69] ". . . officia religiosa, quae in Religione clericali officia ecclesiastica stricto sensu videntur. . . . Conferunt namque modis satis variis 'aliquam participationem' iurisdictionis ecclesiasticae (cf. C. 145, § 1). Sic Superiores sunt propriarum ecclesiarum rectores, vice parochorum funguntur quoad sacramenta, funeralia aliaque centum."—"De Potestate Dominativa Publica in Iure Canonico"—*Acta Congressus Iuridici Internationalis,* IV, pp. 165-166, and note (51).

[70] Cf. canon 145, § 2.

[71] Not an ecclesiastical penalty in the strict sense for the chapters under consideration here have dominative power only and cannot inflict any ecclesiastical penalty. If there is question of depriving a superior of office for any of the crimes in the fifth book of the Code (e. g., canons 2412-2414) this can be done only by some superior with ecclesiastical jurisdiction.

CHAPTER VI

THE CONVOCATION OF THE RELIGIOUS CHAPTER

Canon 162: § 1. Salvis peculiaribus constitutionibus vel consuetudinbus, collegii praeses, statuto modo, loco ac tempore electoribus convenienti, convocet omnes de collegio; et convocatio, quando personalis esse debet, valet, si fiat vel in loco domicilii aut quasi-domicilii vel in loco commorationis.

§ 2. Si quis ex vocandis neglectus et ideo absens fuerit, electio valet, sed ad eius instantiam debet, probata praeteritione et absentia, a competente Superiore irritari, etiam secuta confirmatione, dummodo iuridice constet recursum saltem intra triduum ab habita notitia electionis fuisse transmissum.

§ 3. Quod si plures quam tertia pars electorum neglecti fuerint, electio est ipso iure nulla.

§ 4. Defectus convocationis non obstat, si praetermissi nihilominus interfuerint.

§ 5. Si agatur de electione ad officium quod electus ad vitam retinet, convocatio electorum ante officii vacationem nullum habet iuridicum effectum.[1]

Since the acts of a religious chapter are collegiate acts they must be executed in assembly by vote.[2] It is necessary, therefore, first of

[1] These rules in the Code of Canon Law are directly established for canonical elections, but they should be applied to all the collegiate acts of moral persons. Cf. Maroto, *Institutiones,* I, n. 467; Coronata, *Institutiones,* I, n. 145, p. 172 (note 6); Cappello, *Summa Iuris Canonici,* I, n. 208.

[2] Canon 101, § 1, 1°. Even authors who do not admit that the chapter has a distinct personality, but is a moral person only representatively, say that its acts are collegiate acts and must be performed collegiately. Cf. Coronata, *Institutiones,* I, n. 535; Larraona, "Commentarium Codicis"—*CpR,* VI (1925), 429; Fanfani, *De Iure Religiosorum,* n. 64; Schaefer, *De Religiosis,* p. 232.

all that the chapter be assembled. This is done by the act of convocation. The present chapter of this study will treat of the nature of this act, of what is necessary in order that it may be legitimate, and of the remedies provided in law for neglect of convocation.[3]

ARTICLE I. THE NATURE OF THE ACT OF CONVOCATION

A. The Law Governing the Convocation of the Chapter

§ 1. Salvis peculiaribus constitutionibus vel consuetudinibus. . . .

The prescriptions of law contained in this canon governing convocation are primarily supplementary, for the canon itself makes provision for particular constitutions and customs. The word "*constitutionibus*" as used here embraces any written particular law, i. e., Rules and Constitutions, statutes, chapter decrees, legitimate privileges, etc.; and under the word "*consuetudinibus*" come any accepted practices having the notes of custom, even if, strictly speaking, they would not be juridic customs, e. g., when they pertain to a college not capable, according to canon 26, of introducing a custom.[4] It is, therefore, principally by such constitutions and customs that the convocation of the religious chapter is governed, even if they be contrary to the prescriptions of this canon since they are expressly provided for as demanded by canons 5 and 6, 1°. Before all else, then, in determining any point concerning convocation, the constitutions and customs of the religious institute must be examined and only when the point in question is not provided for in these sources is it to be determined according to the prescriptions of common law contained in this canon.

[3] The expression "neglect of convocation" may seem unusual in English and not be readily understood by the reader. The writer's excuse for using it is that he considers it a technical term which eliminates a constant use of circumlocution. The term is explained in Article IV of the present chapter.

[4] Cf. Larraona, "De Electionibus Religiosorum"—*CpR*, IX (1928), 113 (note 71).

B. The Notion of Convocation

The convocation of a religious chapter may be described as: An authoritative announcement of a chapter to be held by which all those who have the right of active suffrage or the right to be present are notified to assemble at a definite place at a definite time in order to decide, in some definite manner, a matter within the competence of the chapter. This description contains all the requisites for a legitimate act of convocation. The *active subject,* the authority competent to convoke the chapter, is noted in the word *authoritative.* The *passive subject,* those who must be notified, are all those who have either the right of active suffrage or merely the right to be present. The *essential* note of the act of convocation is the *notification to assemble.* The *necessary circumstances* are the *matter* to be treated, the *manner* in which it is to be decided, and the *time* and *place* where the chapter will be held.[5]

C. Species of Convocation

Considering the source from which it comes the convocation may be: (1) *from the law itself,* when in the constitutions, statutes, or legitimate customs of the religious institute the time, place and other necessary circumstances are so determined that those who have the right to be summoned are sufficiently informed concerning the celebration of the chapter and are notified by the law to assemble; (2) *from a superior,* when the convocation emanates from a competent superior. Considering the manner in which the convocation is addressed to those who have the right to be notified, the convocation may be: (1) *general,* when the notification of the chapter is made by a general announcement, e. g., posted in a public place, published in official organs, announced in community, etc.; (2) *personal,* when it is directed to an individual having the right to be notified.[6]

[5] For other descriptions which do not seem sufficiently comprehensive, cf. Aloisius a S. Francisco Paulano, *De Capitulis,* p. 12; Larraona, "De Electionibus Religiosorum"—*CpR,* IX (1928), 329; Fanfani, *De Iure Religiosorum,* n. 102.

[6] There are other species of convocation such as *oral* or *written, to the present* or *to the absent,* etc.; but they are either of no juridical importance or their terms are self-explanatory.

D. The Contents of the Act of Convocation

. . . statuto modo, loco ac tempore electoribus convenienti. . . .

Primarily the act of convocation is directed toward obtaining the assembly necessary for collegiate action, but it also serves the purpose of imparting to those who have either the right of suffrage or the right to be present at the chapter the information that is necessary so that they may exercise their right. This present section will endeavor to establish the points that must be mentioned in the act of convocation so that this right will not be violated and the acts of the chapter exposed to the remedies established in the law for neglect of convocation.[7]

(1) *The notification to assemble.* It is clear from the primary purpose of convocation that it must contain a notification or invitation to assemble. Must this be *formally* expressed? There seems to be no reason to demand such a formal expression. As long as they, who have the right, are informed that a chapter will be held together with the necessary circumstances so that they have knowledge sufficient to enable them to exercise their right, they are sufficiently notified or invited.[8]

(2) *The time and the place of the chapter.* Since it is altogether necessary if one is to exercise his right of suffrage that he should be informed of the place and the exact time (not only the day but also the hour) of the chapter, failure to mention either of these would be equivalent to neglect.[9] However, if either the place or the time or both were already determined by the constitutions or customs so that they were known to those who constituted the chapter, there would be no need of special mention of them in the actual convocation.

(3) *The reason for the chapter.* Must the reason for the chapter, that is to say, the matter to be decided by the chapter be men-

[7] Cf. canon 162, §§ 2-3.

[8] Larraona, "De Electionibus Religiosorum"—*CpR,* IX (1928), 330 (note 81).

[9] Larraona, *loc. cit.*; Coronata, *Institutiones,* I, n. 229, 4°; Maroto, *Institutiones,* I, n. 468, (A); Parsons, *Canonical Elections,* p. 105.

tioned in the act of convocation? The law as established in the Code does not touch this point nor do the authors give this particular question much attention.[10] It seems that the point ought to be decided by employing the same line of reasoning as is used in the other parts of this section. If from the constitutions or customs those who have the right of suffrage already know the reason for the chapter, it would not be necessary to mention it in the act of convocation. If it is not known then it must be declared, for if a voter does not know what matter is to be decided in chapter he has not sufficient information so that he may decide whether or not he wishes to make use of his right; sometimes he would not even be able to exercise it. This becomes clear if the case is considered in which vote by letter is permitted. What purpose would be served by informing a voter of the time when he must vote and of the place to which he should send his vote, if he is not informed upon the question concerning which he is to vote? Therefore, it seems that it would be necessary to include in the act of convocation the reason why the chapter is convoked if it is not already known.

(4) *The manner in which the chapter will reach its decision.*[11] Ordinarily the manner or mode in which the chapter will decide the matter in question need not be mentioned in the act of convocation, for it will either have been determined by the constitutions or customs of the religious institute or the norm established in canon 101 will be followed. In either case it will be known by those who have

[10] Zitelli-Natali (*Apparatus Iuris Ecclesiastici* [Romae, 1907], n. 492) say it would be opportune to specify the reason. Aloisius a S. Francisco Paulano (*De Capitulis*, p. 12) and Pejška (*Ius Canonicum Religiosorum*, p. 216) seem to think it should be mentioned.

[11] The word *modo* in the canon is variously interpreted by authors. Coronata (*Institutiones*, I, n. 288) understands it as designating the manner of convocation; likewise Maroto (*Institutiones*, I, n. 468), yet in another place (n. 615) he clearly interprets this term as referring to the manner of acting in chapter. Larraona ("De Electionibus Religiosorum"—*CpR*, IX [1928], 112) also interprets it in this latter sense. Because of its close connection with *loco ac tempore*, which certainly refer to the actual election (and as has been said to any collegiate action) it seems the word *modo* must be interpreted as referring to the manner of coming to a decision. The manner of convocation will be discussed in a later section of the present chapter.

the right of suffrage and they will, therefore, be sufficiently informed so that they may exercise their right. If, however, some extraordinary manner of arriving at a decision is to be used, which those who constitute the chapter could not be presumed to know and which, if they were ignorant of it, would prevent the exercise of the right of suffrage, then it would be necessary to mention it in the act of convocation, since omission of this necessary knowledge would be neglect. For example, if in the ordinary practice those who had the right of suffrage could vote by letter, but on this occasion the right is restricted to those who are actually present at the celebration of the chapter, failure to mention this would surely amount to neglect of convocation.

As the canon clearly states, the determination of the manner, the time and the place of the chapter is not left entirely to the good pleasure of the superior. He must always take into consideration the convenience of the capitulars.

E. The Necessity of Convocation

§ 4. Defectus convocationis non obstat si praetermissi nihilominus interfuerint.

This section of the canon makes it quite clear that convocation is not *absolutely* necessary for a legitimate chapter, but only *relatively,* that is, so that the presence of those who have the right of suffrage is obtained or, at least, could be obtained. Thus there would be no need for convocation if all the members of the chapter were already actually present.[12] Convocation, moreover, is not *formally* necessary, that is, by an express act of convocation. Any equivalent act or fact, by which those possessing the right of suffrage are adequately notified is sufficient.[13] Finally, convocation is not necessary for the validity of the chapter, as is clear from the canon, but

[12] Cf. Coronata, *Institutiones,* I, nn. 145, 229; Larraona, "De Electionibus Religiosorum"—*CpR,* IX (1928), 330; Maroto, *Institutiones,* I, nn. 468, 616.

[13] Parsons, *Canonical Elections,* p. 104; Coronata, *Institutiones,* I, nn. 145, 228; Maroto, *Institutiones,* I, n. 616; Larraona, "De Electionibus Religiosorum" —*CpR,* IV (1928), 330 and note (81).

it is necessary for what might be called the justice of the chapter; for the right of a voter is certainly violated if he is not summoned when he can be and wishes to be present at the chapter.[14] This gives him the right to attack the acts of the chapter and have them rescinded; and if more than a third of those having the right of suffrage are so neglected the acts of the chapter are *ipso iure* invalid.[15]

Within the limits just expressed it can be said that, generally speaking, convocation is necessary. For in order that the members of the chapter may be enabled to convene in the place where the chapter is celebrated or send their vote by letter, when this is permitted, they must be notified of the chapter to be held and of the necessary circumstances.[16] It must be kept in mind, however, that convocation is governed principally by the constitutions and customs of the particular religious institute. If these prescribe formal convocation, then this prescription would have to be observed. Such prescriptions would not be invalidating unless this sanction were expressly or equivalently stated in the provisions themselves.[17]

F. Juridic Effect of Convocation

The juridic effect of a convocation that has been legitimately made is twofold. In the first place it eliminates any possibility of employing the legal remedies established in law for neglect.[18] Secondly, it confers the exclusive right to vote upon those who are actually present at the celebration of the chapter, saving, of course, the prescriptions of particular law which may demand a definite number or proportional part of the capitulars to constitute a valid chapter or may grant the right to vote by letter or by procurator.[19]

[14] Larraona, *loc. cit.;* Coronata, *Institutiones,* I, nn. 145, 229, also p. 172, note (6).

[15] Canon 162, §§ 2-3. Cf. Article IV of this chapter.

[16] Maroto, *Institutiones,* I, n. 616; Larraona, *loc. cit.;* Coronata, *Institutiones,* I, p. 172, note (6).

[17] Canon 11.

[18] Coronata, *Institutiones,* I, n. 145; Maroto, *Institutiones,* I, n. 467.

[19] Canon 163.

Article II. The Subject of Convocation

I. The Active Subject

. . . collegii praeses, . . . , convocet. . . .

The active subject of convocation, that is, the authority competent to convoke the chapter, may be either the *law itself* or some designated *superior*. If by the particular constitutions or customs of the religious institute those persons who would constitute the chapter are already sufficiently informed and notified to assemble, then the prescriptions of common law that the presiding official of the college should issue the convocation can be disregarded for the chapter is convoked by the law itself.[20] In like manner if the particular constitutions and customs designate the person who is to convoke the chapter this prescription of the Code does not bind.[21] It is only when these particular constitutions and customs do not determine how the chapter is to be convoked that the prescription of this canon is to be observed. The canon says that the superior competent to issue the convocation is the *collegii praeses*. Does this mean the superior of the moral person represented by the chapter or the official who actually presides at the celebration of the chapter? This question is important, for according to common law they can be different persons, and in some chapters of elections in institutes of women religious, they are actually different persons.[22] It seems that the superior competent to convoke the chapter, the *collegii praeses,* is the superior of the moral person and not the official actually presiding at the celebration of the chapter. The principal argument supporting this opinion is drawn from a decision of the Sacred Congregation for Religious. This question was asked of the Sacred Con-

[20] Cf. Larraona, "De Electionibus Religiosorum"—*CpR,* IX (1928), 330-331; Coronata, *Institutiones,* I, n. 229.

[21] Coronata, *loc. cit.;* Larraona, *op. cit.,* 113, 333; Maroto, *Institutiones,* I, nn. 468, 617.

[22] Cf. canon 506, §§ 2, 4. Compare also canon 162, § 1: ". . . collegii praeses . . ." with canon 171, § 1, ". . . cum praeside, si et ipse e gremio collegii sit . . ." and § 2, ". . . coram praeside electionis. . . ."

gregation. Whether the right to determine the place where the general chapter shall be held belongs to the Ordinary of the place where is located the principal house of a religious congregation of diocesan law which has already spread to several dioceses; or whether that right belongs rather to the Superioress General. The Sacred Congregation replied: In the negative to the first part, in the affirmative to the second, according to canons 162 and 507.[23] It need hardly be remarked that this is not an authentic interpretation of canon 162, since the Sacred Congregation for Religious is not competent to interpret authentically the canons of the Code: it is, however, an authoritative decision for religious. The question and response decide only one point, the superior competent to determine the place of the chapter, and that person is declared to be the superior of the moral person; but when the Sacred Congregation says that it has decided according to canon 162 it clearly shows that the *collegii praeses*, according to its mind, is the superior of the moral person and not the official who actually presides at the chapter. This seems to be the only possible meaning of the clause, "according to canon 162." [24] Resting on this principle, then, it may be said that the superior competent to convoke the local chapter is the local superior; to convoke to provincial chapter, the provincial superior; to convoke the general chapter, the Moderator General.[25]

The superior competent to convoke the chapter must abide by the prescriptions of particular law which treat of the convocation of the chapter, either in regard to asking the advice or getting the consent of his council beforehand, or in regard to the time and manner of, as well as the reasons for, convoking the chapter. If the con-

[23] *AAS,* XIII (1921), 481. Translation from Bouscaren, *Canon Law Digest,* I, pp. 279-280.

[24] For the reasons for this decision Cf. Maroto, "Annotationes"—*CpR,* II (1921), 322-329.

[25] Unless the constitutiones declare otherwise, it seems quite probable, because of their superior authority that the Moderator General could convoke a provincial and local chapter and the provincial a local chapter. For according to canon 502 the Supreme Moderator has power over all provinces and houses; and other superiors have authority within the limits of their office, so a provincial would have power over all houses of his province.

stitutions or customs do not prescribe anything in regard to the time, place and manner, he must, nevertheless, take into account the convenience of the capitulars.[26]

Can any other than a competent superior convoke the chapter? Wernz-Vidal say that if any other person besides a competent superior issues the convocation it has no juridic effect, for the act of convocation is an act of jurisdiction or preeminence which no one can usurp.[27] This is surely the correct answer, for no one would be obliged to pay any attention to the act of an incompetent person.

What is to be done if the competent superior refuses to convoke the chapter? A distinction must be made. If the particular law were to leave it entirely to the will of the superior to convoke or not to convoke the chapter, then nothing could be done since he would merely be making use of a right conferred on him by law. It would be an altogether different matter if the chapter were prescribed by the constitutions or customs, as it practically always is. Authors, in treating this point in regard to elections, say that the superior should be requested to convoke the electors, and if he still refuses to do so the right passes to his vicar or the next ranking member of the electoral body, and so on down the line in order of precedence. Moreover, if the time limit for the expiration of the right to elect is imminent and all efforts to obtain a legitimate convocation have failed, the voters can come together without formal convocation lest they be deprived of their right to vote.[28] This devolution of power to an inferior, if it can be justified, is quite unique. Certainly it is not provided for in this canon treating of convocation, nor is it supported by analogy with other cases of devolution in the Code; there we find that power, which was not used when it should have been or was used wrongfully, devolves upon one having superiority in

[26] Canon 162, § 1; Chelodi, *Ius de Personis,* n. 138; Maroto, *Institutiones,* I, nn. 468, 619; Coronata, *Institutiones,* I, nn. 228, 229; Larraona, "De Electionibus Religiosorum"—*CpR,* IX (1928), 113.

[27] *Ius Canonicum,* II, n. 252.

[28] Cf. Maroto, *Institutiones,* I, n. 617, and p. 734, note (1); Larraona, "De Electionibus Religiosorum"—*CpR,* IX (1928), 334; Coronata; *Institutiones,* I, n. 229; Parsons, *Canonical Elections,* p. 100.

regard to the power neglected or misused.[29] So also, it seems, should this case be handled. If the chapter is prescribed and the legitimate superior refuses to convoke it, recourse should be had to the superior of the person who refuses to do what is lawfully required of him.[30] If there is not time to have this recourse and the chapter could assemble under a legitimate president it would be lawful to do so, since lack of convocation is no obstacle to the celebration of a legitimate and valid chapter.[31]

II. The Passive Subject

. . . omnes de collegio. . . .

A. *They Who Must Be Called*

The word *collegium* here must be taken in a somewhat different sense from that signified in the section above treating of the active subject of convocation. There the word was understood as denoting the moral person represented by the chapter, here the word must be taken as denoting the collection of physical persons who by law compose the chapter; that is, those persons who, according to law, enjoy the right of active suffrage or the right to be present at the chapter whether they are actually members of the moral personality represented or not.[32] That this is the true meaning of *collegium* in

[29] Cf. Canon 161; 178; 182; 274, 5°; 432, § 2; 434, § 3; 1432, § 3. It should be noted that the question discussed here concerns only a power not used or wrongfully used; when the superior is legitimately impeded or the office vacant the power does sometimes devolve upon an inferior, e. g., canon 429.

[30] Cf. Piat, *Praelectiones,* I, p. 654.

[31] Cf. canon 162, § 4, and Article I, E, of this Chapter.

[32] The two clauses "the right to be present at the chapter" and "whether they are actually members of the moral personality or not" were included in the meaning of *collegium* because such cases actually happen. Thus the Ordinary of the place has the right to be present and preside in certain elections of women religious (canon 506, §§ 2, 4), and so is really a member of the *collegium* but he is not a member of the moral personality represented nor does he have the right of suffrage. A Superior General presiding with the right of suffrage in a provincial chapter is not a member of the moral person represented but is certainly a member of the *collegium*. Cf. Aloisius a S. Francisco Paulano, *De Capitulis,* p. 14.

this place is clear from the reasons of the convocation. Convocation is the ordinary means for obtaining the assembly necessary for the collegiate acts of moral persons, and it is those only who have the right of active suffrage or the right to be present who can constitute such an assembly. It would be useless, then, to call to the assembly those who have no right of suffrage or no right to be present. Convocation is, moreover, a protection granted to those who possess these rights, so that if they lose these rights through neglect of convocation, the collegiate action is either rescissible or *ipso iure* invalid.[33] On this ground, also, the convocation would be useless for those who do not possess these rights, since they have no rights to protect. On the other hand, it would be very necessary for everyone who had these rights whether he were a member of the moral person represented or not, and in either case he could employ the legal remedy for loss of his right through neglect. If it be objected that it is not a reasonable interpretation of law to take the same word in the same sentence in two different senses, it can be answered that it is the only way to reconcile an interpretation based on the obvious ends of the law with an interpretation based on an authoritative decision.

Who are they who possess the right of active suffrage or the right to be present and must, therefore, be called to the chapter? In general it may be said that this is not determined by common law but must be gathered from the particular constitutions and customs of each religious institute. There are, however, some points of common law which ought to be mentioned since they have a bearing on this subject:

(1) In chapters of nuns for the election of the superioress, the Ordinary of the place where the chapter is to be held must always be notified since he has a right not only to be present but also to preside.[34]

(2) In the same chapters the regular superior must also be notified if the nuns are subject to him.[35]

(3) In chapters for the election of the Superioress General in

[33] Canon 162, §§ 2-3.
[34] Canon 506, § 2.
[35] Canon 506, § 2.

congregations of women religious the Ordinary of the place where the chapter is to be held must be notified since he has the right to be present and to preside.[36]

(4) Negatively the Code declares that those who are only temporarily professed do not enjoy the right of active suffrage. Provision is made in the canon, however, for contrary prescriptions of the constitutions.[37]

(5) The time prescribed for enjoying electoral rights, when the constitutions are silent on this point, is to be reckoned from the first profession.[38]

In the pre-Code common law there were some restrictions in regard to the right of suffrage which are not in the law of the Code and, therefore, according to the norm of canon 6, 6 °, they must be considered as abrogated unless they are found in the sources constituting particular law. These are:

(1) In clerical institutes a religious had to have at least the order of subdiaconate in order to have the right of suffrage.[39]

(2) A woman who entered an institute in which two of her sisters were already members lacked active and passive suffrage.[40]

Before the present legislation went into effect it was the common teaching that the superior was not bound to summon all who had the right of suffrage but only those *qui debent et volunt et possunt commode interesse.* Canonical opinion is divided as to whether this is still tenable.[41] In order to determine whether or not this teaching of the pre-Code authors can still be followed it seems better to consider it part by part rather than as a unit, since in this way a more satisfactory solution can be reached.

(1) *Qui debent interesse.* The word *debent* here is not to be taken in an obligatory sense but facultatively, that is, it denotes a

[36] Canon 506, § 4.

[37] Canon 578, 3°.

[38] Canon 578, 3°.

[39] Council of Trent, sess. XXII, *de ref.*, c. 4. Augustine (*A Commentary*, III, 109) denies that such a restriction ever existed in regard to religious chapters.

[40] S. C. Ep. et Reg., 3 iun. 1701—Bizzarri, p. 336. Cf. "Questions Answered" —*Review for Religious* (St. Mary's, Kansas: St. Mary's College, 1942—), I, 422 (hereafter cited as *RfR*).

[41] Cf. Parsons, *Canonical Elections*, pp. 101-102.

right to be present not an obligation.[42] Thus the doctrine of the pre-Code authors was that only those who had the right to be present had to be summoned and those who had no right, either because they never had it or because they had in some way lost the use of it, need not be summoned. Certainly, even under the present legislation, no obligation can be placed on the superior to summon those who have no right to be present.

(2) *Qui volunt interesse.* If there is question of a right that one can renounce and actually has renounced, provided he has never retracted his renunciation, it certainly does not seem reasonable to impose on the superior the obligation to summon him. However, since a man's will is changeable, it would be prudent on the part of the superior to have the renunciation made in a form that could be used juridically, that is, executed either in writing or before witnesses.[43] If there is question of a right that one may not renounce, then the superior certainly should summon every capitular.[44]

(3) *Qui commode possunt interesse.* If, without any fault on the part of the superior, the capitular cannot possibly be present, there would be no obligation on the part of the superior to summon him; for, in this case, his absence could not be attributed to the neglect of the superior. If it were merely inconvenient for the capitular to be present, then he ought to receive the invitation; because even if it were inconvenient for him and he still wished to avail himself of his right but could not because he had not been notified, he would certainly be neglected and could avail himself of the remedy provided by law.

The question is proposed by several authors whether one who is not a member of the chapter could be called and given the right of suffrage. In answering this question they distinguish between chapters of election and other chapters. Because of the prohibition of canon 165, they say that anyone extraneous to the college, saving legitimate privileges, cannot be admitted to the election. For other chapters they say that by the unanimous consent of the capitulars

[42] Wernz-Vidal, *Ius Canonicum,* II, n. 252, note (23).

[43] Wernz-Vidal, *Ius Canonicum,* II, n. 252, note (23).

[44] Larraona, "De Electionibus Religiosorum"—*CpR,* IX (1928), 336, note (104).

one who is not a member of the chapter could be called and given the right of suffrage.[45] The latter part of this solution does not seem to be sound. The necessary qualifications for possessing the right of suffrage in chapter are determined by the constitutions of the institute and to give this right to one who does not have these qualifications seems to be changing the constitutions. Hence, unless the constitutions expressly permit this or the superior issuing the convocation has the power to change the constitutions in this respect, no one who is not a member of the chapter can be called and given the right of suffrage.[46]

B. *They Who Need Not Be Called*

It will not be out of place, for the purpose of completeness, to consider as briefly as possible those persons whom the superior need not summon. In the first place there are those persons who are extraneous to the college, that is, those persons who do not possess the necessary qualifications demanded by the constitutions for enjoying the right of active suffrage.[47] Then there are those persons who, while they possess the qualifications, cannot validly exercise this right. These are called in the Code those who cannot vote.[48] The Code groups them in five classifications.

(1) *They who have become incapable of a human act.*[49] The only case of this kind is that of those persons who have been afflicted with a serious mental disorder, e. g., insanity. Strictly speaking they do not lose their right of suffrage, but are merely incapable of exercising it.[50] Hence if they should have recovered their mental fitness at the time of convocation they should be summoned to the chapter.[51]

(2) *They who have not reached the age of puberty.*[52] Under the present legislation it is highly improbable, if not impossible, that

[45] Piat, *Praelectiones,* I, p. 656; Aloisius a S. Francisco Paulano, *De Capitulis,* p. 31.

[46] Cf. Goyeneche, "Consultationes"—*CpR,* VII (1926), 390-392.

[47] Canon 165. Cf. Parsons, *Canonical Elections,* pp. 116-119.

[48] Canon 167, § 1.

[49] Canon 167, § 1, 1°.

[50] Maroto, *Institutiones,* I, n. 622.

[51] Aloisius a S. Francisco Paulano, *De Capitulis,* pp. 33-34.

[52] Canon 167, § 1, 2°.

anyone who has not reached the age of puberty will have the other qualifications required for active suffrage in a religious chapter. However, if by dispensation someone were permitted to join a religious institute and make religious profession before the age of puberty, they would still be incapable of voting because of the prescription of this canon.[53]

(3) *They who are bound by censure or infamy of law after declaratory or condemnatory sentence.*[54] A censure is an ecclesiastical penalty by which one, who is baptized, guilty of crime and contumacious, is deprived of some spiritual goods or goods connected with spiritual things until, abandoning his contumacy, he is absolved.[55] Specifically the ecclesiastical censures are excommunication, suspension and personal interdict.[56] Infamy of law is loss of one's good repute inflicted by the law itself in cases expressly stated in the common law.[57] It is a vindicative penalty. Consequently it does not cease with absolution from the crime because of which it was contracted but only by dispensation conceded by competent authority, which in regard to infamy of law is the Apostolic See alone.[58] A declaratory sentence is that by which a judge pronounces that the guilty party has certainly transgressed a law or precept to which a penalty *latae sententiae* has been attached and was not excused from contracting this penalty by any legitimate cause.[59] A condemnatory

[53] Exception must be made for canon 526 which, in the matter of the reappointment of the ordinary confessor, gives the right of voting to all, even if they lack it in other matters.

[54] Canon 167, § 1, 3°.

[55] Canon 2241.

[56] Canon 2255. Suspension applies only to clerics (canon 2255, § 2) and, therefore, not to lay religious.

[57] Canon 2293, § 2.

[58] Cf. canon 2236, § 1; 2295.

[59] Cf. canon 2242, § 2; 2223, § 4. The crimes punished in the Code with a censure or infamy of law *latae sententiae* are too numerous to relate here. They can be found listed systematically in many works on canon law and moral theology. E. g., for censures *latae sententiae,* cf. Woywod, *A Practical Commentary on the Code of Canon Law* (2 vols., 5. ed., New York: Wagner, 1939), Appendix II (hereafter cited as Woywod, *Practical Commentary*); for infamy of law, cf. Arregui, *Summarium,* n. 904.

sentence is that by which a judge inflicts a penalty *ferendae sententiae* on a party who is guilty of violating a law or precept to which such a penalty is attached, when he has not amended after judicial warning.[60] It is to be particularly noted that the mere commission of the crimes to which such penalties are attached does not make one incapable of casting a valid vote, but only after a legitimate sentence does one become incapable.[61] How far does this inability extend, to elections only or also to other affairs expedited by vote? Certainly it applies to the right to vote in any election conducted in a religious chapter and not only to elections to an ecclesiastical office strictly so-called.[62] Since it cannot be clearly shown that it applies also to the right to vote in other capitular affairs, it cannot be so extended since it is a penal matter and must be strictly interpreted.[63]

(4) *They who have given their name or publicly adhered to an heretical or schismatical sect.*[64] Although it was at one time disputed it is now certain from a response of the Pontifical Commission for the Authentic Interpretation of the Code [65] that this legal incapacity does not apply to those persons who come into the Church from the heresy or schism in which they were born, but solely to those who fall away from the faith and join a non-Catholic sect.[66] Since this crime is already punished in the law with the penalty of infamy of law it may be asked why it is repeated here. The reason seems to be

[60] Cf. canons 2223, §§ 2-3; 2233, § 2; 2242, § 2.

[61] Exception must be made for one who has laid violent hands on the person of the Sovereign Pontiff for such a one is *excommunicatus vitandus* without any declaration (canon 2243, § 1, 1°).

[62] Cf. Parsons, *Canonical Elections,* p. 123. The prohibition of canon 2265, § 1, however, applies only to elections to an ecclesiastical office in a strict sense. Parsons, *loc. cit.*

[63] Cf. canons 19, 2219.

[64] Canon 167, § 1, 4°.

[65] October 16, 1919—*AAS,* XIV (1919), 477.

[66] A later response of the Commission declared that atheistic sects were to be regarded as equivalent to non-Catholic sects—July 30, 1934—*AAS,* XXVI (1934), 494. These two responses were not given as an interpretation of canon 167 but as interpretations of the similar phrase *sectae acatholicae* of canon 542, 1°. There can be no doubt that they apply equally to canon 167. Cf. Vermeersch-Creusen, *Epitome,* I, n. 245; Coronata, *Institutiones,* I, n. 231.

that because of the enormity of this crime it is set down as involving legal incapacity even prior to the rendering of judicial sentence.[67]

(5) *They who lack active suffrage either because of the legitimate sentence of a judge or because of a prescription of common or particular law.*[68] The meaning of the word *carentes* in this section of canon 167 is not clear. Some say it must be understood as to both sources of incapacity in a penal sense only, that is, as including both classes of those incapacitated by this section of canon 167 only those "deprived of the right of some crime." Parsons [69] treats the question at length and concludes that it must be understood as referring to penal deprivation only. In his argument from the context he says: "But a still stronger argument is found in the context of n. 5 itself Two phrases depend on the one word *carentes,* namely, *carentes ob legitimam sententiam* and *carentes ex iure communi.* The word, *carentes,* is not repeated and must, therefore, bear the same meaning in both cases; but those who have no vote because of a judicial sentence are certainly 'penally deprived.' Therefore, those who have no vote because of common or particular law are such as are penally deprived by common or particular law." This argument does not seem sufficiently cogent. The phrases in question are clearly separated by the disjunctive particles *sive . . . sive.* Why, then, could not the word, *carentes,* be understood in its general denotation of "lacking" and take on a penal connotation when understood with the first phrase and a penal or non-penal connotation when understood with the second, depending on the nature of the law establishing the privation? Moreover, as Parsons himself remarks, this is the only place where the Code could include the non-penal privations of active voice. If these privations be excluded here it would seem that there could be religious lacking the right of active voice and yet capable of casting a valid vote; for example, the cardinals and bishops spoken of in canon 629. This is avoided if the word, *carentes,* be understood, when taken in with the phrase, *ex iure communi aut particulari,* in a penal or non-penal sense depending on the nature of the law. This

[67] Aloisius a S. Francisco Paulano, *De Capitulis,* p. 40.

[68] Canon 167, § 1, 5°.

[69] *Canonical Elections,* pp. 125-127.

does not seem to be doing violence to the text of the law, but seems rather to be its obvious meaning. It must not, however, be so far extended as to include those who lack the essential requisite qualities for the right of suffrage. These are already excluded by canon 165.

The religious who, not guilty of crime, lack active suffrage from common law are: (1) the exclaustrated during the time of the indult of exclaustration;[70] (2) cardinals and bishops who have laid aside their prelacy and returned to their religious institute.[71]

The religious who, guilty of crime, lack active suffrage from common law are:

(a) *after legitimate sentence:* (1) they who have conspired against the authority of the Roman Pontiff, his legate or their own ordinary;[72] (2) they who pass laws, mandates or decrees against the liberty or rights of the Church;[73] (3) they who have recourse to any lay power to impede the exercise of ecclesiastical jurisdiction;[74] (4) they who join a masonic or like sect;[75] (5) religious men of solemn vows who admit women into the cloister;[76] (6) they who fabricate or falsify letters, rescripts, or decrees of the Holy See or knowingly use such false documents;[77] (7) they who are guilty of the crime of solicitation;[78] (8) they who violate the sacramental seal;[79] (9) and they who violate the common life in a notable matter;[80]

(b) *ipso facto:* apostates from religion, who are perpetually de-

[70] Canon 639. Practically all authors seem to consider this as a penal privation. This does not seem to be justified. If a religious with no fault on his part finds it necessary to seek an indult of exclaustration, where is the delinquent to be corrected and the crime to be punished? Without delinquency there can be no ecclesiastical penalty. Cf. explanation of ecclesiastical penalty in canon 2215.

[71] Canon 629.

[72] Canon 2331, § 2.

[73] Canon 2334, 1°; 2336, § 1.

[74] Canon 2334, 2°; 2336, § 1.

[75] Canons 2335, 2336, § 1.

[76] Canon 2343, 2°.

[77] Canon 2360.

[78] Canon 2368, § 1.

[79] Canon 2369, § 1.

[80] Canon 2389.

prived of active suffrage even after they have returned to their obedience.[81]

The question may also be asked whether the privation of active suffrage attached by common law to certain crimes is to be extended to all matters decided by suffrage or only to elections. Pre-Code authors were divided on this question.[82] Modern authors do not treat this question expressly. To the present writer there seems to be no reason to restrict this privation to the right to vote in elections. When using the term *vox activa* in the law for religious, the Code of Canon Law does not distinguish between the right to vote in elections and the right to vote in other chapter affairs.[83] That the right to vote in other capitular affairs is included in the phrase *vox activa* as used in the Code can be gathered from sources given by Cardinal Gasparri in which there is question of the right to vote for the admission of a religious to solemn profession.[84] This is confirmed by canon 526 where the right of suffrage, though it is not called *vox activa,* clearly embraces other matters besides elections. Since, then, in the Code itself and in the pre-Code law the term *vox activa* does include other capitular affairs besides elections and since in the various canons where the privation is established it is never restricted to electoral rights, in the interpretation of the privation it must be considered to include the deprivation of the right of suffrage in every capitular business expedited by voting. This may seem a very theoretical question but it could have very practical consequences. Suppose, by way of example, that the consent of the local chapter were required for admission to first profession [85] and the novice obtained but one vote over the required majority. If one of the capitulars favoring admis-

[81] Canon 2385. There are other crimcs because of which electors are deprived of the right of electing but they have no relation to the subject under discussion here.

[82] Cf. Piat, *Praelections,* II, p. 610.

[83] Cf. canons 578, 3°; 629; 639. These are the only places that the term is used in the law for religious.

[84] In footnote to canon 578, 3°: S. C. super Statu Regularium, 7 febr. 1862—*Fontes,* n. 4387; S. C. Ep. et Reg., decr., *"Perpensis,"* 3 maii 1902, n. 8—*Fontes,* n. 2039.

[85] As it is, e. g., in the Congregation of the Passion. Cf. Aloisius a S. Francisco Paulano, *De Capitulis,* p. 18.

sion had been deprived of active suffrage, such a novice would be invalidly admitted to profession and the religious profession itself would be invalid.[86]

C. *The Obligation Imposed By Convocation*

It has been shown that all and only those members of the religious institute who are capable of exercising the right of active suffrage or who have merely the right to be present must be summoned to the chapter, it now remains to consider the question whether the convocation imposes on them an obligation to be present. May one renounce his right and so absent himself from the chapter? A clear cut answer to this question is rather difficult. The principal difficulty lies in the nature of the right of active suffrage. If it is a right that is conceded for the public good, it does not seem that one may renounce it, inasmuch as it imposes a duty that one must fulfill. If it is a right given in one's own favor, it seems it may be renounced since in this case it would be equivalent to a personal privilege given in one's own favor.[87] Certainly if the particular law of the institute imposes an obligation of obeying the convocation or of using the right of active suffrage the religious has no choice. According to Larraona, such particular laws are rather common among religious.[88] Likewise if the official who issues the convocation is truly a superior he could add to the convocation a precept which could even be confirmed by a sanction under the vow of obedience.[89] Moreover, an obligation, either from justice or charity, that one should make use of one's right could arise under special circumstances; e. g., if one should foresee that because of his renunciation an unworthy person would be elected, a statute harmful to the institute would be passed, a damaging contract would be entered into, etc.[90] Prescinding, however, from such

[86] Cf. canon 575, § 2 and canon 572, § 1, 2°.

[87] Cf. canon 72, § 2.

[88] "De Electionibus Religiosorum"—*CpR*, X (1929), 56 and notes (114), (115).

[89] Larraona, *loc. cit.* Cf. Aloisius a S. Francisco Paulano (*De Capitulis*, p. 48) who relates several occasions when St. Paul of the Cross, founder of the Passionists, actually added such precepts obliging under the vow of obedience.

[90] Larraona, *loc. cit.*; Aloisius a S. Francisco Paulano, *De Capitulis*, p. 114, note (2); Fanfani, *De Iure Religiosorum*, n. 102.

obligations arising from the prescription of particular law, from a precept, or from circumstances, does the very nature of the right of suffrage and convocation suppose a strict obligation to obey the convocation and to be present at the chapter? Larraona says that the common opinion, both before and after the Code, is that the right of suffrage does not impose a duty but gives a faculty which one may renounce.[91] This seems to be the mind of the Code also, for it establishes the privation of the right of active suffrage as a vindicative penalty,[92] that is, a penalty that is established directly for the expiation of a crime,[93] and one is not usually deprived of a duty imposed for the public good to expiate a personal crime.

Article III. The Circumstances of Convocation

A. *The Manner of Convocation*

... et convocatio, quando personalis esse debet, valet, si fiat vel in loco domicilii aut quasi-domicilii vel in loco commorationis.

The common law has not enacted any prescription in regard to what might be called the accidentals of the manner in which the chapter is to be convoked, e. g., whether it must be in writing or *viva voce*, by circular letter, publication, etc. These points, therefore, are either determined by the particular constitutions or customs of the institute, or, if such prescriptions of particular law are lacking, left to the discretion of the superior who is competent to convoke the chapter.[94] The manner chosen by the superior must, however, be such that under ordinary circumstances the knowledge of the fact that the chapter is to be held will come to those who have a right to

[91] *Loc. cit.* He admits that men of great authority hold that the right of suffrage is given not for one's own benefit but for the common good and hence a duty obliges one to use the right for the purpose for which it was given.

[92] Canon 2291, 11°.

[93] Canon 2286.

[94] Vermeersch-Creusen, *Epitome,* I, n. 243; Chelodi, *Ius de Personis,* n. 138; Maroto, *Institutiones,* I, nn. 468, 619; Fanfani, *De Iure Religiosorum,* n. 102; Coronata, *Institutiones,* I, n. 228.

be present and in sufficient time to permit them to be present.[95] The only point that is determined in common law is what is sufficient when the convocation must be personal. The question to be settled here is when the convocation must be personal. Fanfani seems to demand that all the absent should receive a personal summons.[96] Blat says the summons must be personal either because of circumstances or because of prescription of law.[97] This much is certain, if there is a prescription of particular law that some persons should receive a personal summons, that prescription must be observed. Moreover, from the canon itself this seems to be the only case when the convocation must be personal. For from the tone of the canon the personal convocation is indicated as something exceptionally obligatory *(quando personalis esse debet)*. Now no one is obliged to make use of an extraordinary means unless such an obligation is clearly proved. There seems to be no other source from which, in our case, such an obligation could arise except the definite prescription of law.[98] Therefore it must be said that general convocation is sufficient and personal convocation is not required or subject to being demanded unless it is prescribed by law.[99]

Presuming, then, that the obligation to issue a personal convocation is proved, how would it be fulfilled in regard to summoning the members of a religious chapter? The canon says that it is sufficient if it be made in one of three places—domicile, quasi-domicile or place of actual residence. Religious do not have a domicile or quasi-domicile

[95] Parsons, *Canonical Elections*, p. 104; Coronata, *Institutiones*, I, n. 228; Maroto, *Institutiones*, I, n. 619; Fanfani, *De Iure Religiosorum*, n. 102.

[96] *Loc. cit.*

[97] *Commentarium Textus Codicis Iuris Canonici*, 5 vols. in 7, Vol. II, *De Personis* (2. ed., Romae: Libreria del Collegio Angelico, 1921), n. 106 (hereafter cited as Blat, *Commentarium*).

[98] An example of such a prescription of particular law demanding a personal convocation is found in the Constitutions of the Swiss-American Congregation of Benedictines in which all the absent must be notified by registered letter of the holding of a chapter for the election of a new abbot.—*Declarations on the Holy Rule and Constitutions of the Swiss-American Congregation, O.S.B.* (Conception Abbey, Conception, Mo.: Altar and Home Press, 1938), n. 104.

[99] Larraona, "De Electionibus Religiosorum"—*CpR*, IX (1928), 332 and notes (89), (90).

strictly so-called, but they do have places of abode analogous to them. Analogous to a domicile for religious would be the house to which they have been assigned and analogous to a quasi-domicile would be the place to which they have been sent for some special purpose, e. g., a university to pursue studies or to teach. If, then, the convocation were made in either of these places or in the place where the religious were actually residing, it would be sufficient for a personal convocation. A personal convocation need not be made in the presence of him, who must be summoned personally, but it is sufficient if a letter be addressed to him.[101] A practical way, but one not required,[102] to make sure that any convocation, either general or personal, which is made by letter, reaches its destination is to send it by registered mail requesting a return receipt.

B. *The Time and the Causes of Convocation*

The common law establishes no particular prescriptions about the time when a religious chapter should be convoked or about the causes why it should be convoked. This is no oversight because in the Schema of the Code published in 1916 it was prescribed that in regard to the time when chapters—general, provincial or local—were to be celebrated the constitutions of each institute were to be observed.[103] This was omitted in the final edition because it was thought to be so evident that it was not necessary to state it.[104] Hence for the time when a religious chapter is to be convoked, as well as for the causes which demand capitular action, the constitutions of each institute must be consulted. It will be well, however, to take note here of some prescriptions of common law which have bearing on the time when religious chapters, particularly chapters of election, should be convoked.

(1) *In regard to all chapters.* The convocation must be issued at such time as will leave a sufficient interval to permit every capitular

[100] Larraona, *op. cit.*, 322, note (91).

[101] Maroto, *Institutiones*, I, n. 619.

[102] Unless prescribed by particular law as in the case of the Swiss-American Benedictine Congregation mentioned above.

[103] *Schema Codicis Iuris Canonici* (Romae, 1916), canon 509, § 1.

[104] Aloisius a S. Francisco Paulano, *De Capitulis*, p. 15.

to arrive in time for the celebration of the chapter if he wishes to do so. For if the convocation sets a date that does not give the capitulars sufficient time to appear it is regarded as invalid,[105] that is to say, those capitulars who could not arrive in time are considered as neglected.[106]

(2) *In regard to chapters of election for all offices.* According to the prescription of canon 161 every college of electors, which in the present case is a religious chapter, must exercise its right of election to fill an office within three months from the time the office becomes vacant under pain of losing its right to elect. As a necessary consequence the chapter must be convoked in sufficient time to permit the chapter to complete the election within the prescribed time.

(3) *In regard to chapters of election for an office which is held for an indefinite period.*

§ 5. Si agatur de electione ad officium quod electus ad vitam retinet, convocatio electorum ante officii vacationem nullum habet iuridicum effectum.

This section of canon 162 mentions directly only offices which are held for life, but the norm here established should also be applied to any office which does not become vacant through lapse of a predefined time.[107] It declares that any act of convocation before an office is actually vacant has no juridic effect. Therefore, if a chapter of election were convoked before the office became vacant and a new act of convocation were not issued after it actually became vacant and, as a result of this omission, some of the capitulars were not actually present, the election would be subject to the remedies for neglect of convocation.[108]

[105] Maroto, *Institutiones,* I, n. 615; Pejška, *Ius Canonicum Religiosorum,* p. 216; Parsons, *Canonical Elections,* p. 104.

[106] Coronata, *Institutiones,* I, n. 229.

[107] Maroto, *Institutiones,* I, n. 613.

[108] Cf. Parsons, *Canonical Elections,* p. 107. Maroto (*Institutiones,* I, n. 468) applies this rule to all the collegiate acts of moral persons and says that convocation cannot be made before the matter to be settled can be treated according to law. As an example, however, he gives the case of election for an office held for life. It is rather difficult to see to what other business it could apply.

It may be asked, could a religious chapter be convoked at a time or for a cause not provided for in the particular law of the institute? Since, according to canon 501, the chapters possess only the authority given them by the constitutions, if the matter in question has not been committed even implicitly to the chapter by the constitutions it could not be called to decide the question since this would involve changing the constitutions. The same answer must be given in regard to times not provided for in the constitutions.[109]

Article IV. Neglect of Convocation and the Legal Remedies

§ 2. Si quis ex vocandis neglectus et ideo absens fuerit, electio valet, sed ad eius instantiam debet, probata praeteritione et absentia, a competente superiore irritari, etiam secuta confirmatione, dummodo iuridice constet recursum saltem intra triduum ab habita notitia electionis fuisse transmissum.

§ 3. Quod si plures quam tertia pars electorum neglecti fuerint, electio est ipso iure nulla.

§ 4. Defectus convocationis non obstat, si praetermissi nihilominus interfuerint.

A. *The Notion of Neglect and the Persons Who Are Considered Neglected*

Neglect as used in law in respect to convocation may be described as any defect in the convocation which is imputable to the superior who is responsible for the convocation and which directly results in the absence of some capitular.[110] Inability to exercise the right of suffrage which, by reason of the prescription of particular law, could be exercised by letter or by proxy, must be considered as equivalent to this physical absence. It must be noted particularly that the defect must be imputable to the superior who has the right and the duty to issue the convocation; hence, when the convocation is completely made by the law itself there can never be any question of neglect.

[109] Cf. Aloisius a S. Francisco Paulano, *De Capitulis*, p. 16; *Normae* (1901), art. 206-210.

[110] Coronata, *Institutiones*, I, n. 229.

This neglect can arise either from fraud, that is, a deliberate will not to summon, or from simple negligence for which the superior is responsible.[111] If the superior has done all that is required of him, that is, has issued the convocation in the ordinary manner and carried out all the prescriptions of law, common and particular, and still some were not informed, this can in no way be imputed to the superior and there can be no question of neglect. The defects in convocation that lead to the absence of some of the capitulars can arise from various sources. Thus convocation can be defective:

(1) On the part of the superior who convokes the chapter, when it has not been issued by a competent authority. This is a complete lack of convocation.[112]

(2) On the part of the time when it was issued; that is, if it were not issued according to the requisites in regard to time.[113]

(3) On the part of the manner, if a personal convocation were not made when it should have been personal or if the manner prescribed by law were not observed.

(4) On the part of the contents, if something necessarily to be known in order to be present were omitted.[114]

B. *The Effects of Neglect.*

Neglect of convocation in itself is not penalized in the law. This is very clear from § 4 of the canon, which declares that defect of convocation is no obstacle if those who were neglected were actually present. It is, therefore, only when the neglect is joined with actual absence that the law supplies a remedy. Two conditions, then, are necessary: (1) actual absence; (2) due directly to neglect of convocation. It is clearly evident that the absence of any capitular can be attributed directly to neglect of convocation, only when some defect in the convocation is the sole reason why he was not present. A question here presents itself. If one of the capitulars were not legitimately summoned, but from some other source he obtained all

[111] Coronata, *loc. cit.*

[112] Cf. Article II, I of this chapter.

[113] Cf. Article III, B.

[114] Cf. Article I, D.

the information necessary so that he could have been present but still was not, could the chapter be contested on the grounds of neglect? *Salvo meliori iudicio,* to the present writer it seems that it could not; for, even if the summons should have been personal, if the capitular had all the requisite information and still did not take the steps necessary to exercise his right, his absence cannot be attributed causatively to the lack of convocation, as the particle *ideo* seems to demand, but must be attributed to his own free choice.

C. *The Legal Remedies for Neglect*

When the two conditions mentioned above are present, the law declares that the chapter can be invalidated by the competent superior or is *ipso iure* invalid.

(a) *When the chapter can be invalidated.* If one or more of the capitulars, up to and including one third of the whole body entitled to receive notice, have been neglected and as a consequence were absent, the chapter is valid but at the instance of any neglected party it must be invalidated by the superior. This is called an *actio de contemptu.* It is a personal action and, therefore, it can be introduced only by someone who has actually suffered the injury and by no one else.[115] If more than one have been neglected it is not necessary that all of them should introduce it; introduction by any one of them is sufficient. No one is obliged to make use of this remedy; he may simply ratify the capitular action by not making use of this remedy supplied him by law. If, however, he does wish to make use of this remedy he must do so within three days. As the canon states, this time is to be reckoned not from the time he was neglected or from the time of the chapter, but from the time the knowledge of the celebration of the chapter came to him. As long as he can prove juridically that he has made recourse within the time alloted by law, his petition must be allowed. If he fails to institute proceedings within the prescribed time the action ceases by law[116] and the chapter can never again be attacked on the grounds of neglect.

This action can be conducted either judicially or administra-

[115] Coronata, *Institutiones,* I, n. 229; Maroto, *Institutiones,* I, n. 618.
[116] Canon 1702.

tively.[117] If it is conducted judicially, the competent tribunal will be determined according to the prescriptions of common law.[118] If it is conducted administratively the superior competent to receive the recourse is the superior to whom belongs the right to confirm the acts of the chapter, or if the acts of the chapter do not need confirmation, the next superior above the one who has been guilty of neglect, unless the particular law of the institute determines otherwise.[119] If the injured party has recourse within the prescribed time and proves the injury, the canon leaves no choice to the superior; he must invalidate the acts of the chapter.

(b) *When the chapter is ipso iure invalid.* If more than a third of the capitulars were neglected and as a result of the neglect were absent, the capitular actions are null *ipso iure*. Therefore, they cannot be ratified by the injured parties, but must be performed again.

[117] Maroto, *Institutiones,* I, n. 618.

[118] Canons 1557, § 2, 2°; 1573; 1594, § 4.

[119] Cf. Larraona, "De Electionibus Religiosorum"—*CpR,* IX (1928), 339; Pejška, *Ius Canonicum Religiosorum,* p. 221.

CHAPTER VII

THE CELEBRATION OF THE RELIGIOUS CHAPTER

THE celebration of the chapter is the series of actions by which the moral personality manifests its will. It may be described as the complex of things to be done by the capitulars because of the prescriptions of common and particular law so that the decisions of the chapter may be valid and not rescissible.[1] From this description the scope of the present chapter becomes clear. It will be an attempt to indicate what is required on the part of the persons constituting the chapter and on the part of the actions performed by them in order that the capitular decisions may be legitimate and endowed with this necessary stability. Finally there will be a short treatment of the defects that may occur in these acts.

ARTICLE I. THE CAPITULARS

A. *Who Must Be Admitted and Excluded*

This question has already been sufficiently discussed in the treatment of the passive subject of convocation.[2] It need only be remarked here that all and only those who, according to the prescriptions of common and particular law, have the right to be present must be admitted, and all and only those who have the right of suffrage must be permitted to vote. Supposing, however, that one or more of the capitulars, although they have been legitimately summoned, are unjustly excluded or ejected or unjustly prevented from voting, does the law supply any remedy for this injustice? Some authors [3] consider such persons as neglected and absent in the sense of canon 162 and authorized, therefore, to make use of the legal remedy supplied

[1] Cf. Aloisius a S. Francisco Paulano, *De Capitulis,* p. 51.

[2] Cf. Chapter VI, Article II, II.

[3] E. g., Maroto, *Institutiones,* I, n. 618; Larraona, "De Electionibus Religiosorum"—*CpR,* IX (1928), 331, note (108).

in that canon. Parsons [4] thinks that these cases are not covered by the canons but would permit the same remedies by analogy on the basis of canon 20. This seems a very reasonable solution; for while it is true that one who is unjustly excluded, ejected or prevented from voting could not strictly be said to be *neglectus* or *praetermissus* and consequently *absens,* still the result would be the same, that is, there would be an unjust privation of the same right and therefore the same legal remedy should be permitted.[5]

B. *The Necessity of a Physical Assembly*

An actual physical assembly is not a condition *sine qua non* demanded by the nature of a collegiate act of a moral person, since the only condition absolutely required is that the decision be made by suffrage.[6] However, such an assembly does seem to be always required under the common law.[7] At this place it may be asked whether, since canon 163 permits a vote by letter, this exception can be so far extended that collegiate action can be accomplished entirely by epistolary vote without any physical assembly at all. Maroto [8] thinks it could be so extended and there seems to be no reason to deny this since the canon in making exception for a vote by letter does not restrict it in any way. However, the ordinary way is that the voters should assemble and hence it may be said that as a general rule this assembly is always required for collegiate action.[9]

[4] *Canonical Elections,* p. 193.

[5] This remedy and the method of employing it have already been discussed in Chapter VI, Article IV, C.

[6] Cf. canon 101, § 1; Maroto, *Institutiones,* I, n. 467; Gillet, *La Personnalité Juridique en Droit Ecclésiastique, spécialement chez les Décrétistes et les Décrétalistes et dans le Code de Droit Canonique,* Dissertations ad gradum magistri in facultate Theologica consequendum conscriptae, Series II, Tomus 18 (Malines: W. Godenne, 1927), p. 259 (hereafter cited as Gillet, *La Personnalité Juridique*).

[7] Cf. canon 105, 2°.

[8] *Institutiones,* I, 468, 623.

[9] Maroto, *Institutiones,* 468; Wernz-Vidal, *Ius Canonicum,* II, n. 32. Coronata (*Institutiones,* I, n. 145) requires it for the validity of the action: "Ut actus collegialis sit, generatim omnes de collegio in eundem locum auctoritative designatum convenire debent; haec autem physica adunatio, ex iure communi ad valorem necessaria est nisi aliud probetur."

C. *Physical Presence As a Requisite for Voting*

The common law for elections, and consequently for elections in religious chapters by reason of canon 507, § 1, demands that the voter be physically present at the chapter in order to exercise his right and altogether excludes any vote by letter or proxy unless this is permitted by particular law.[10] The legislative source from which such a *"lex peculiaris"* of canon 163 must come is disputed. As Parsons [11] rightly remarks, there seems to be no reason to attach any special significance to the term *"lege peculiari"* and hence it means any particular law. Therefore, since the canon makes provision for particular law, it makes no difference by what legislative authority it is passed, whether it is written or non-written, whether promulgated before or after the Code. It should be noted, however, if the electoral law is determined by the constitutions, a change to permit a vote by letter or proxy could be made only by an authority competent to change the constitutions.[12] An exception is made in the common law for one who is present in the house where the chapter is celebrated, but, because of illness, cannot be present at the actual celebration of the chapter.[13] The word *"domus"* in canon 168 need not be taken in the strict sense of the physical building but rather any place within the confines of the religious property where the chapter is held.[14] In this case the capitular has a strict right to vote and the tellers must go and obtain his vote in every ballot that is cast, unless, as the canon states, it is otherwise provided by particular law or legitimate custom.[15]

Does this requisite of common law that one must be physically present in order to vote apply also to collegiate actions other than

[10] Canon 163.

[11] *Canonical Elections,* p. 89.

[12] Parsons, *Canonical Elections,* pp. 112-113.

[13] Canon 168: "Si quis ex electoribus praesens in domo sit in qua fit electio, sed electioni ob infirmam valetudinem interesse nequeat, suffragium eius scriptum a scrutatoribus exquiratur, nisi aliter particularibus legibus vel legitimis consuetudinibus fuerit constitutum."

[14] Parsons, *loc. cit.*

[15] Canon 168.

elections? Michiels [16] says that it does and that no consideration is to be given to the absent even if they send their vote by letter unless this is permitted by particular law. This seems to be true, for these rules, although they are directly established for elections, are also the common law for all matters expedited by suffrage.[17] Hence, unless the particular law of some institute permits the right of suffrage to be exercised by letter or proxy, only they who are actually present at the chapter can vote on any matter coming before the chapter.

D. *The Necessity of a Quorum*

A quorum is the minimum number of persons without which there can be no valid collegiate action. It may be established either numerically (e. g., at least three persons) or proportionately (e. g., at least two thirds of those having suffrage). The only situations in which a quorum is required by common law are when no convocation is issued and when more than a third of those having the right of suffrage are neglected in the convocation. In either of these two cases two thirds of the capitulars are required for valid collegiate action, since according to canon 162, § 3 if more than a third were neglected and as a consequence were absent the action is *ipso iure* invalid.[18] When, however, the convocation has been legitimately issued the common law requires no definite number of the capitulars, either numerically or proportionately, for valid collegiate action. Canon 163 says that the right of suffrage belongs to those only who are present on the day set for the chapter in the convocation. Hence, if even only one were present the right to make the decision would rest entirely with him. In this regard also the prescriptions of particular law would have to be observed. The *Normae,* for example, required two thirds of the capitulars for a valid general chapter.[19]

[16] *Principia Generalia de Personis in Ecclesia* (Belgium: Braaschaat, 1932), pp. 383-384 (hereafter cited as Michiels, *Principia Generalia de Personis*).

[17] Thus canon 697, § 2 says: "In iis quae ad convocationem ad comitia et electiones respiciunt, serventur ius commune, quod prostat in can. 161-182. . . ." Cf. also canon 20.

[18] Maroto, *Institutiones,* I, n. 468.

[19] Art. 223.

Hence constitutions modeled on the *Normae* will likewise require two thirds of the capitulars for a valid general chapter. As is quite evident, the only way to determine whether in some particular institute a quorum of any kind is required is to consult its particular laws. In examining these laws it should be particularly noted whether they prescribe such a quorum only to open a chapter validly, or also at all times for every capitular action. If it be required only for beginning the chapter, then, if some capitulars afterwards departed, they who remained could continue to act validly, unless a majority had decided to postpone the chapter.

E. *The Concession of One Vote to Each Voter*

Canon 164: Etsi quis plures ob titulos ius habeat ferendi nomine proprio suffragii, non potest nisi unicum ferre.

This canon clearly prescribes that in elections each voter may cast only one vote in his own name. One cannot admit the opinion proposed by Goyeneche [20] that if one can cast more than one vote in his own name because of a single title he may be permitted to do so since the canon forbids the casting of more than one vote because of several titles. This opinion is based on an erroneous reading of the canon. The canon says that a voter cannot cast more than one vote *even if* he has the right to vote because of several titles—the obvious conclusion seems to be that *a fortiori* this would be forbidden if he had but a single title.[21] A voter may, however, cast more than one vote if the additional votes are cast by reason of his being a proxy, since such votes would not be cast in his own name. This canon makes no provision for contrary prescriptions of particular law; hence no particular law can derogate from it unless it be pontifical law promulgated after the Code.

The present writer has been able to find no author who raises the question whether this canon should be applied to collegiate actions other than elections. Since these canons, as has been remarked,

[20] "Consultationes"—*CpR,* VIII (1927), 31.

[21] Cf. Parsons, *Canonical Elections,* p. 115.

contain the common law on voting it seems that it should be extended to such actions and so, *salvo meliori iudicio,* in no capitular action may anyone be permitted to cast more than one vote in his own name.

ARTICLE II. THE OFFICIALS

A. *The Presiding Official*

Although the Code in treating of collegiate actions usually makes mention of a presiding official,[22] it nowhere prescribes that the presence of such an official be regarded as necessary for validity of the collegiate action.[23] Ordinarily the person who presides is the same as he who convokes the chapter.[24] In order to determine definitely in any particular religious institute to whom the right to preside belongs the particular law of the institute must be consulted. The common law determines the presiding official in two cases.

(1) In the election of the superioress of a monastery of nuns.

> **Canon 506: § 2. In monasteriis monialium, comitiis eligendae Antistitae praesit, quin tamen clausuram ingrediatur, Ordinarius loci aut eius delegatus cum duobus sacerdotibus scrutatoribus, si moniales eidem subiectae sint; secus, Superior regularis; sed etiam hoc in casu Ordinarius tempestive moneri debet de die et hora electionis, cui potest una cum Superiore regulari per se ipse vel alium assistere et, si assistat, praeesse.**

Two possibilities are considered in this canon; either the nuns are subject to the local Ordinary or they are subject to a superior of an institute of men of solemn vows. In the first case the canon prescribes that the local Ordinary, either in person or by delegate, should preside at the election of the superioress. In the second case the canon confers on the local Ordinary the right to be present, either in person or by delegate, and, if he does assist, also to preside. In

[22] E. g., canons 105, § 1; 171; 174; 397, 4°; 506, §§ 2, 4.

[23] Parsons, *Canonical Elections,* p. 134; Coronata, *Institutiones,* I, n. 233.

[24] Cf., e. g., canon 397, 4°; Aloisius a S. Francisco Paulano, *De Capitulis,* p. 56.

both cases he must be seasonably informed of the day and hour of the election. In both cases, whether he be present in person or by delegate, he presides with full right of jurisdiction and not as enjoying merely an honorary chairmanship.[25] If the local Ordinary does not wish to preside when the nuns are subject to a regular superior, the regular superior has the obligation to preside.

(2) In the election of the General Superioress of a congregation of women religious.

> **Canon 506: § 4. In mulierum Congregationibus electioni Antistitae generalis praesideat per se vel per alium Ordinarius loci, in quo electio peragitur; cui, si agatur de Congregationibus iuris dioecesani, peractam electionem confirmare vel rescindere integrum est pro conscientiae officio.**

This section of canon 506 prescribes that the local Ordinary, either in person or by delegate, should preside at the election of any General Superioress of a congregation of women religious conducted within the confines of his territory. In congregations of pontifical approval the law does not confer on him any rights in regard to the confirmation of the elected superioress. In congregations of diocesan approval he has the right to confirm or rescind the election according to his conscience. The canon restricts his right to preside to the election of the General Superioress, and when this has been legitimately completed, his duties cease. The right to preside at any further elections or capitular business belongs to the person designated by the particular law. Usually the newly elected Superioress will preside.[26]

The common law nowhere details exhaustively the definite duties of the presiding official. It does prescribe that he is to sign the acts,[27] and announce the election.[28] It also confers on him sometimes the

[25] Cf. the two responses of the Pontifical Commission for the Interpretation of the Code on this canon: 24 nov. 1920—*AAS,* XVIII, 393; 30 iul. 1934—*AAS,* XXVI, 494.

[26] Cf. *Normae* (1901), art. 224.

[27] Canon 171, § 5.

[28] Canon 174.

duty and sometimes the right to settle a tie vote.[29] His duties, however, are evident from his very position. He is to direct the deliberations of the chapter so that they may proceed in an orderly manner and according to the prescriptions of law. These duties may be more definitely described in particular law.

B. *The Scrutineers or Tellers*

Canon 171: § 1. Ante electionem per secreta suffragia deputentur, nisi iam propriis statutis deputati sint, e gremio collegii duo saltem scrutatores. . . .

Before every election by ballot the common law requires that at least two scrutineers or tellers be appointed. If the particular law requires more than two, this specific provision would have to be observed since it is not contrary to the Code which merely establishes the minimum number that must be appointed. As the canon notes, they must be members of the electoral body. The election of the superioress in a monastery of nuns is an exception to this rule since, according to the prescription of canon 506, § 1, the tellers in this election must be priests. It is their duty to collect the votes and, together with the presiding official, to count, examine and tabulate them.[30] They also must sign the acts of the election.[31] The manner of appointing the tellers is sometimes certain, sometimes doubtful.

(1) It is certain from the very prescription of the canon that if the tellers are already appointed by the proper statutes of the electoral college, nothing further is required in the way of appointment and those so designated fulfill this office.

(2) It is equally certain that in the election of a superioress of a monastery of nuns subject to the local Ordinary, he alone has the right to designate the scrutineers. He is not permitted, however, to appoint the ordinary confessors of the nuns for this office.[32]

(3) It is also certain that when the regular superior actually

[29] Canon 101, § 1, 1°. This point will be discussed later.

[30] Canon 171, § 2.

[31] Canon 171, § 5.

[32] Canon 506, § 3.

presides over nuns who are subject to him he appoints the scrutineers, with the limitation just noted in the case of appointment by the local Ordinary.

(4) It has been disputed whether this right belongs to the local Ordinary or to the regular superior when the local Ordinary presides at the election of nuns who are subject to the regular superior. It is unquestioned that before the Code the regular superior had the right to appoint the tellers.[33] However, this pre-Code practice was based on the teaching that the local Ordinary had a presidency of honor and direction, while the presidency of jurisdiction belonged to the regular superior. This can no longer be held since the Pontifical Commission for the Interpretation of the Code has declared that the local Ordinary has a true presidency of jurisdiction.[34] Hence it seems that under the present legislation the local Ordinary has the right to appoint the scrutineers.[35]

(5) The final case is had when it is not an election of a superioress of a monastery of nuns and the scrutineers are not already appointed by the proper statutes. How are the tellers to be appointed in this case? Eliminating, for the sake of clarity, the clause containing the exception, the canon, which determines that tellers should be appointed, reads: *"Ante electionem per secreta suffragia deputentur e gremio collegii duo saltem scrutatores . . ."* The difficulty lies in the words, *per secreta suffragia*. Should they be understood as modifying the word, *electionem*, and thus determine the kind of election in which tellers are necessary; or should they be understood to modify the verb, *deputentur*, and so determine the manner in which they should be chosen? It does not seem that any conclusive argument in support of either opinion can be drawn from the Latin word order, especially in a sentence involving an inverted word order such as is present in this case. The reason, then, from "structural balance" by which Parsons [36] attempts to support the opinion that the canon determines the manner of appointing the scrutineers, need not be

[33] Cf. Larraona, "Commentarium Codicis"—*CpR*, VIII (1927), 26-27, note (348).

[34] 30 iul. 1934—*AAS*, XXVI, 494.

[35] Cf. Parsons, *Canonical Elections*, pp. 136-137.

[36] *Canonical Elections*, p. 146.

taken very seriously. It is at least counterbalanced by this consideration, that if the legislator wanted the phrase in question to modify *electionem,* it stands in the only place in which he could have put it. The majority of authors, it is true, hold that the tellers must be appointed by the secret vote of all the capitulars present,[37] but since their interpretation cannot be proved to be the correct one it seems safe to follow the opinion of Coronata [38] that the canon does not determine the manner of appointing the tellers and so the accepted practice of any electoral body may still be followed; if there is no accepted practice or custom then the chapter can appoint them but is not necessarily bound to do so by secret suffrage. Scrutineers are not required for collegiate actions other than election by ballot. In such elections, however, they are an essential part of the form.[39]

C. *The Secretary*

Canon 171: § 5. Omnia electionis acta ab eo, qui actuarii munere fungitur, accurate describantur, . . .

In all elections there is to be a secretary appointed whose duty it is to write down accurately all the acts of the election. The law does not determine how he is to be appointed; this will be determined by the practice of each institute. The law does not require that he be one of the electors, nor does it prescribe his presence as a condition for the validity of the election.[40] He also must sign the acts of the chapter. It is quite clear that a secretary will be equally useful for all capitular business.

D. *Other Officials*

Sometimes the particular law of religious institutes prescribes that certain other officials be appointed—masters of ceremony, hebdomadaries, guardians of the chapter room, interpreters, etc. The necessity of such officials, the manner in which they are to be appointed, and

[37] Cf. Parsons, *Canonical Elections,* p. 145, and authors cited in note (41).
[38] *Institutiones,* I, n. 234.
[39] Parsons, *loc. cit.*
[40] Coronata, *Institutiones,* I, n. 233.

their duties can be determined only by consulting the particular laws of each institute.[41]

Article III. Preliminary Actions

A. *The Determination of the Time and the Place of the Chapter*

Enough has already been said on the subject of the time when a religious chapter should be convoked in the chapter on the convocation of the chapter and the reader is referred to what has already been said.[42] The common law determines no specific place for the holding of any religious chapter and if the particular law does not determine the place, it belongs to the superior who issues the convocation to do so. This superior, as has already been noted, is the superior of the moral personality represented by the chapter and not necessarily the person who presides at the actual celebration.[43]

B. *Prayers*

The common law prescribes no prayers or religious exercises either in preparation for or during the actual celebration of the chapter. This is usually done by the particular laws and customs of each institute. What religious exercises are prescribed, as well as when, how and by whom they are to be conducted can be learned only by consulting the sources which constitute the particular law of each society.

C. *The Presentation of Credentials and Documents*

The common law does not prescribe any presentation of credentials as a requisite for participation in a religious chapter. A person delegated to preside at a religious chapter should certainly present to the chapter his mandate or letters of delegation.[44] Since it is the duty of the presiding official to see that all things are done according to

[41] Cf. Parsons, *Canonical Elections,* p. 138; Aloisius a S. Francisco Paulano, *De Capitulis,* pp. 87-88.

[42] Chapter VI, Article III, B.

[43] Cf. Chapter VI, Article II, I.

[44] Aloisius a S. Francisco Paulano, *De Capitulis,* pp. 74-75.

the prescriptions of law, upon him will rest the principal obligation to investigate the authorization enjoyed by those present and see that each has the right to participate. Any prescriptions of particular law in this matter will have to be observed. If a doubt arises whether some individual is qualified, Maroto [45] says that authors, relying on many decisions of the Sacred Roman Rota, usually settle it in this way. If the person cannot prove that he has the qualifications required by law, he is not to be admitted since he cannot established his right to participate. On the other hand, if it is known that he has the qualifications and it cannot be proved that he has ever been deprived, then he must be admitted since he is in possession of the right and cannot be deprived of it except for a certain cause.

Formerly no superior could validly vote in the election of major superiors of regulars unless he could testify that all Mass obligations had been satisfied or could be satisfied in a short time. This is no longer required by common law.[46] The presentation of a document attesting to this, as well as documents attesting to the faithful keeping of the archives, the financial condition of the house or province and the like may still be required by particular law,[47] but they are not to be considered as requisites for participation in the chapter unless this is clearly proved.

D. *The Official Opening*

Usually the presiding official opens the chapter in some formal way. How this is to be done is determined by the accepted practice in each institute. Certainly, since it is now clearly established who is to be admitted and excluded, it is no longer necessary for the presiding official to make the official protestation that the chapter does not wish to admit any who have no right to be present or to exclude any who are qualified.[48]

[45] *Institutiones,* I, n. 629.

[46] Parsons, *Canonical Elections,* p. 141.

[47] Aloisius a S. Francisco Paulano, *De Capitulis,* pp. 76-81.

[48] Aloisius a S. Francisco Paulano, *De Capitulis,* p. 74. In the same place the author outlines the procedure for the formal opening of provincial and general chapters among the Passionists.

E. *Oaths*

(1) The Oath of the Presiding Officials and Tellers

Canon 171: § 1. . . . duo saltem scrutatores, qui una cum praeside, si et ipse e gremio collegii sit, iusiurandum interponant de munere fideliter implendo ac de secreto servando circa acta in comitiis, etiam expleta electione.

As the canon clearly prescribes it is only when the presiding official and the tellers are members of the chapter that they are obliged to take this oath. Hence when the local Ordinary or a regular superior presides in election of women religious, or when priests act as tellers in such elections, they do not take this oath. In all other elections, even in institutes of women religious, when the presiding official and the scrutineers are members of the chapter they are obliged by the prescription of this canon. The oath is twofold: (1) it obliges them to perform their duty faithfully; (2) it obliges them not to reveal, even after the election is completed, what was done in the election. The oath of secrecy does not, of course, forbid the tellers to publish the results of the balloting since this is part of their duty,[49] nor does it oblige them to keep secret what it would be permissible for other voters to reveal. It obliges them particularly not to reveal any knowledge which they acquire exclusively in the exercise of their office and which others have no right to obtain.

(2) The Oath of Electors

Canon 506: § 1. Antequam ad Superiorum maiorum electionem deveniatur in religionibus virorum, omnes et singuli e Capitulo iureiurando promittant se electuros quos secundum Deum eligendos esse existimaverint.

This oath is obligatory in institutes of men religious only. The authors say that women religious are excluded lest they be troubled by scruples and anxieties of conscience.[50] Whether this be the reason

[49] Canon 171, § 2.

[50] E. g., Larraona, "Commentarium Codicis"—*CpR,* VII (1926), 447.

or not matters little, the point to be noted is that the common law does not impose the obligation on women. Even in societies of men the oath is not obligatory in all elections, but only in elections of major superiors. The Code has determined the meaning of the term "major superior" among religious. Major superiors are the abbot primate, the abbot superior of a monastic congregation (ordinarily called the abbot praeses), the abbot of a monastery *sui iuris,* the provincial superior, all who are vicars of those already mentioned, and others having power equivalent to that of provincial superiors.[51] The oath obliges those who take it to one thing only, that they will elect the person whom before God they think should be elected. In simpler words it obliges them to follow the dictates of their conscience in their choice of a superior. As Parsons[52] very well notes, if the opening ballot shows that a voter's choice has no chance of election, it would be better for him to shift his vote to the one he deems best fitted among the candidates having a possibility of being elected. Naturally, there would be no obligation to do this, unless by continuing to vote for the person the voter thinks should be elected he would be assisting in the election of someone who was really unfit. This oath would first of all oblige the voters to elect a person having the qualifications demanded for the office by common[53] and particular law, unless they have good reason for making use of postulation.[54] The combination of moral, intellectual and administrative talents that

[51] Canon 488, 8°.

[52] *Canonical Elections,* p. 140.

[53] E. g., canon 504 requires that major superiors be born of legitimate marriage, ten years professed from first profession, and forty years of age in the case of the Supreme Moderator and thirty years of age in the case of other major superiors.

[54] In regard to postulation it is advisable to keep in mind the declaration of the Sacred Congregation for Religious: ". . . whenever a real ineligibility exists on any legal grounds grave reasons are required for a dispensation. Hence, the simple will of the voters or the fitness of the person is not a sufficient reason for the dispensation" (9 mar. 1920)—*AAS,* XII, 365 (translation from Bouscaren, *Canon Law Digest,* I, 276). This letter was issued in regard to the repeated re-election of Supreme Moderators in congregations of women religious, but it can be taken as an expression of the mind of the Sacred Congregation in regard to all postulation.

go to make up the ideal religious superior cannot be determined by rules, but is a matter that depends on the judgment and experience of the voters and in this, particularly, each voter must be guided by the dictates of his conscience.

(3) Other Oaths

The two oaths already considered are the only ones prescribed by common law for religious chapters. Others can be and are prescribed by particular law. What these are and by whom they must be taken can be learned only from an investigation of these particular laws.[55]

(4) Manner of Taking Oaths

No formula for an oath is prescribed by the common law, hence any formula may be used unless one is prescribed by the particular law. In regard to the manner of taking an oath, priests take an oath *"tacto pectore,"* all others by placing their hand upon a book containing the Gospels.[56]

F. *The General Absolution*

The general absolution from censures and irregularities is usually imparted in order of regulars and congregations which possess the privilege. At the present time the omission of this ceremony would have no effect on the validity of the election.[57]

[55] E. g., in the provincial and general chapters among the Passionists the guardian of the chapter room is placed under oath of secrecy in regard to anything he may hear in the exercise of his office; all capitulars are under oath not to reveal anything said about the eligible in the discussion of qualifications. Cf. Aloisius a S. Francisco Paulano, *De Capitulis,* pp. 162, 164. In the same congregation all members of the local chapter are bound by an oath of secrecy as regards anything harmful to the character of anyone discovered in the discussion of the fitness of candidates for admission to sacred orders.—*Statuta a Clericis Excalceatis Congregationis SS. Crucis et Passionis D. N. J. C. Servanda* (Romae, 1935), n. 54.

[56] Canon 1622, § 1.

[57] The formula is found in the Roman Ritual, tit. VIII, cap. 33. Cf. Parsons, *Canonical Elections,* p. 141; Maroto, *Institutiones,* I, n. 631; Goyeneche, "Consultationes"—*CpR,* XIV (1933), 262.

G. *The Appointing of Committees*

In provincial and general chapters committees are usually appointed to facilitate the handling of the business to be conducted in the chapter of affairs. These committees hold preliminary meetings in which they discuss the business committed to them, formulate it for presentation to the chapter, and propose reasons for and against its acceptance. The number of such committees as well as the manner in which they are to be appointed will depend on the particular law and accepted practice of each religious institute.[58]

H. *The Preliminary Discussion*

A discussion of the matter in question preliminary to the decision by collegiate action is neither prescribed nor forbidden by the Code. A consideration of the parallel case when a superior must have the counsel or consent of a group of persons leads one to the conclusion that this course of action has the definite approval of the law.[59] Authors in treating of the collegiate actions of moral persons say that a mature and deliberate discussion should precede the decision.[60] In no case, however, is this preliminary consideration required for the validity of collegiate action. The advantage of such an exchange of ideas is very evident for it will always be useful, and at times even necessary, for an intelligent exercise of the right of suffrage. Whether this discussion is to be conducted privately or in common will be determined by the accepted practice in each institute.

It might be well at this point to consider in particular the discussion preliminary to capitular elections in connection with the grave prohibition of canon 507, § 2. This section of canon 507 warns all religious to avoid seeking, directly or indirectly, to procure votes for themselves or for others.[61] In conformity with the spirit of this

[58] Cf. Ellis, "The General Chapter of Affairs"—*RfR*, I (1942), 255.

[59] Canon 105, 2°: ". . . eae personae legitime convocentur, . . . et mentem suam manifestant; . . ." 3°: "Omnes de consensu vel consilio requisiti debent ea qua par est reverentia, fide ac sinceritate sententiam suam aperire."

[60] E.g., Maroto, *Institutiones*, I, n. 468.

[61] "Caveant omnes a directa vel indirecta suffragiorum procuratione tam pro seipsis quam pro aliis."

canon the discussion of the qualifications of candidates should not degenerate into a caucus to procure votes for individuals. Parsons,[62] resting on the reason for this law and the teaching of the classic pre-Code authors, distinguishes very well between good and evil procuring of votes and ably defends the lawfulness of procuring votes for a good end. However, while this procuring of votes for a good end (e. g., to assure the election of the best fitted or to prevent the election of one who is obviously unfit) may be perfectly lawful, it does not seem to be expedient. Human nature being what it is, if some religious set out to procure votes to assure the election of him, whom they think is most worthy, others will do the same, and this useful and often necessary means of communicating information will become a cabal. It would seem better, then, to take the words of the canon strictly and avoid any attempt to procure votes or to persuade others how to vote even with the very best motives.[63] If the discussion is confined strictly to a simple and truthful statement of the qualifications or disqualifications of the eligible without any attempt at persuasion or procuring of votes and the decision is left to the conscience of each voter, where it rightfully belongs, then the purpose of the discussion will be fully attained without any danger of violating the prohibition of this canon. For the sake of clarity, however, it should be noted that the procuring of votes even for an unworthy motive will not invalidate the election or even the votes unless fraud, undue pressure of authority or the like have destroyed the freedom of choice.[64]

Article IV. Capitular Decisions in General

Canon 101: § 1. Circa actus personarum moralium collegialium:

[62] *Canonical Elections,* pp. 190-193.

[63] Larraona ("Commentarium Codicis"—*CpR,* VIII [1927], 111) makes an observation on this point that is very pertinent: "Prohibitio tangit etiam procurationem suffragiorum pro aliis. Et merito nam nemo ius habet sese substituendi iudicio electorum in aestimatione personae aptioris ad munus de quo agatur et insuper agitationes, quae ex procuratione suffragiorum nascerentur absque dubio, vitae religiosae quieti et sanctitati graviter attentarent."

[64] Cf. canon 169, § 1, 1°.

1°. Nisi aliud expresse iure communi aut particulari statutum fuerit, id vim iuris habet, quod, demptis suffragiis nullis, placuerit parti absolute maiori eorum qui suffragium ferunt, aut, post duo inefficacia scrutinia, parti relative maiori in tertio scrutinio; quod si suffragia aequalia fuerint, post tertium scrutinium praeses suo voto paritatem dirimat aut, si agatur de electionibus et praeses suo voto paritatem dirimere nolit, electus habeatur senior ordine vel prima professione vel aetate;

2°. Quod autem omnes, uti singulos, tangit, ab omnibus probari debet.

A. *The Manner of Reaching a Decision*

Nisi aliud expresse iure communi aut particulari statutum fuerit. . . .

This introductory clause makes it quite clear that the manner of reaching a decision in collegiate action established by this canon is a supplementary prescription of law; that is to say, it obliges only when there is not some other manner already provided by common or particular law. The first question that presents itself upon reading this clause is whether a collegiate decision can be reached in some other way than by suffrage. Taken by itself, the clause would seem to allow an interpretation permitting this, but when it is considered in conjunction with the text of the whole paragraph it introduces, such an interpretation is excluded. The whole tenor of the paragraph supposes that the decision is to be reached by the casting of votes and, consequently, is concerned only with determining what portion of the votes is sufficient to constitute a decision. Hence, authors say that the element that is essential and always required for collegiate actions is the act of voting by those members of the moral person who have the right of suffrage,[65] and, as already noted, who are actually present.[66] Hence the *aliud* can refer only to some

[65] E. g., Maroto, *Institutiones*, I, n. 467; Gillet, *La Personnalité Iuridique*, p. 259; Michiels, *Principia Generalia de Personis*, p. 382.

[66] Cf. Article I, C. of this chapter.

other method of computing the portion of the votes requisite for a decision, or to a greater or lesser number of ballots, or to some other way of settling a parity of votes, etc.[67] These diverse prescriptions may be established by common or particular law. Since the canon does not restrict its provision for particular laws in any way, this may be done by any particular law, which, of course, includes legitimate custom.[68] There are only three express prescriptions of common law establishing a norm different from the one here given which are applicable to a religious chapter. (1) In the election of an abbot *nullius* at least an absolute majority of votes is always required; [69] hence, the chapter will have to continue balloting until this majority is obtained by some candidate. (2) An absolute majority of votes is required for valid postulation, and when it concurs with an election two thirds of the votes cast are required.[70] (3) The decision to retain the ordinary confessor in institutes of women religious must be approved by an absolute majority of all the members of the house even of those who do not have the right of suffrage in other affairs.[71] In order to determine whether the particular laws or customs of some religious institute provide norms differing from those given in the canon under consideration the sources of such particular law will have to be consulted.

It has already been noted that the common law does not definitely commit any particular act to a religious chapter, but when this is done by particular law, must that affair be resolved by the vote of the chapter or is it possible that the chapter by vote should merely decide to delegate the solution to some other person or group of persons? Certainly, if an election is in question the chapter can proceed by way of compromise unless the particular law does not

[67] Cf. Michiels, *Principia Generalia de Personis*, p. 393; Coronata, *Institutiones*, I, p. 174, note (5).

[68] Blat (*Commentarium*, II, n. 32) interprets the word *expresse* as excluding custom. Coronata (*Institutiones*, I, p. 176, note 5) rightly remarks that a custom can contain an express disposition of law. Also Michiels, *Principia Generalia de Personis*, p. 392.

[69] Canon 321.

[70] Canon 180.

[71] Canon 526.

permit this.[72] It seems to be the same with any other business committed to the chapter. For if it is committed to it by particular law it would be ordinary power [73] and this can always be delegated unless delegation is expressly prohibited.[74]

B. *The Manner of Voting*

If election by way of scrutiny be excepted,[75] the common law does not establish any norms governing the manner of voting for collegiate action. It is not necessary that the suffrage in collegiate action be a secret suffrage.[76] This may, however, be prescribed by common [77] or particular law for some determined affair, but it will never be required for the validity of the vote unless this is expressly or equivalently stated.[78] One might say that the common law favors a secret vote; [79] and it is always to be recommended since it is one of the greatest safeguards of freedom of choice. Ellis says that all matters of greater importance should be decided by secret ballot and that any member of the chapter may demand a secret ballot on any proposition; it will then be in the discretion of the chapter to decide whether this request is to be complied with.[80]

A very common manner of voting in religious chapters when there are only two possibilities to choose from (e. g., either approval or disapproval) is by the use of marbles, beans, etc.; white for approval, black for disapproval. Each capitular is given one black ballot and one white ballot. The ballot box or urn is passed twice; the first time to collect the votes, the second time to collect the unused ballot. This preserves the secrecy of the ballot. It is quite evident that

[72] Cf. canon 507, § 1 and canon 172.

[73] Canon 197, § 1.

[74] Canon 199, § 1.

[75] Capitular elections will be discussed in the succeeding article.

[76] Cf. Coronata, *Institutiones,* I, n. 145.

[77] E. g., canons 169, 526.

[78] Canon 11. As in canon 169.

[79] Thus it uses the word *scrutinium* in canon 101, a word which carries a connotation of something secret.

[80] "The General Chapter of Affairs in a Religious Congregation"—*RfR,* I (1942), 256.

there would be no need to pass the box a second time if the decision were reached by the unanimous vote of all present. Since the manner of voting is quite definitely settled by the accepted practice of each institute there is nothing to be gained by prolonging a discussion on ways of casting the votes.

C. *The Counting of the Votes*

When the votes have been collected they should first be counted. If the total is equivalent to the number that should have been cast, it is a valid ballot and the votes can be examined to determine the result. It will also be valid if a lesser number have been cast, for the presumption is that some have renounced their right of suffrage. What is to be done if there are more votes than voters? In an election this is an invalid ballot as is clearly stated in canon 171, § 3.[81] This ballot is not to be considered as one of the three permitted by canon 101.[82] Should the same rule be applied to other collegiate actions? The writer has been able to find no author who treats this specific question and is of the opinion that if it does not apply directly, it should be applied by way of analogy since there would be lacking an express prescription of law.[83]

D. *The Determining of the Result*

(1) In Affairs not Affecting the Capitulars as Individuals.

> ... id vim iuris habet, quod, demptis suffragiis nullis, placuerit parti absolute maiori eorum qui suffragium ferunt, aut, post duo inefficacia scrutinia, parti relative maiori in tertio scrutinio; quod si suffragia aequalia fuerint, post tertium scrutinium praeses suo voto paritatem dirimat aut, si agatur de electionibus et praeses suo voto paritatem dirimere nolit, electus habeatur senior ordine vel prima professione vel aetate;

[81] "Si numerus suffragiorum superet numerum eligentium, nihil est actum."
[82] Cf. Parsons, *Canonical Elections*, p. 151.
[83] Canon 20.

The majority necessary for a decision is to be computed in relation to the total number of valid votes, for the canon makes it clear that votes that are null are not to be counted (*demptis suffragiis nullis*). Those votes only will be invalid which have been expressly or equivalently declared to be so by law, hence the prescriptions of common and particular law in this matter will have to be investigated. As Coronata [84] remarks, general rules cannot be drawn from the prescriptions of law for particular affairs; thus all the requisites for a valid vote in an election by scrutiny should not necessarily be applied to a vote in every collegiate action. In the very nature of things a blank vote, a vote cast by one incapable of a human act, a vote cast by one not in possession of the right of active suffrage, a vote that is not certain and determined, etc., will be invalid. Because of the prescription of law a vote that is extorted by force or fear is always invalid. [85] More specific requirements will have to be drawn from the prescriptions of law in particular affairs.

The canon clearly determines that the majority is to be computed in relations to the number of votes actually cast (*qui suffragium ferunt*) and not in relation to the number of voters present or to the total number who have a right to vote. Here also the prescriptions of particular law could determine otherwise and demand that the majority be computed in relation to the number who have a right to vote.

On the first and second ballot an absolute majority is required for a decision. An absolute majority is any number exceeding half of the votes (e. g., four out of seven). If on neither of these ballots an absolute majority was obtained, then on the third ballot a relative majority will suffice. A relative majority is had by the part having more votes than any other. By way of example, if seven votes were cast and two possible solutions obtained two votes each, and a third solution obtained three votes, the third would have a relative majority. The smallness of the number is of no consideration in a relative majority as long as it is greater than the number cast for any other possible solution. As is quite clear, a relative majority

[84] *Institutiones,* I, n. 145.
[85] Canons 103, § 1; 169, § 1, 1°.

is possible only when there are more than two possible solutions, for if there be only two possible solutions the relative majority will be likewise an absolute majority.

It can happen that a decision will not be reached even on the third ballot because two or more possible solutions have obtained an equal number of votes. When an equality of votes is obtained in an action other than an election it is the practically unanimous opinion of authors that the president of the college *must* decide which of the conflicting solutions having a parity of votes shall be adopted.[86] Maroto,[87] apparently, is the only author who defends the position that the word *dirimat* in the canon is not preceptive but facultative. The common opinion is supported by the fact that the law has established no alternative method of reaching a decision in these affairs as it does for elections. The assertion of Maroto that the college may leave the business undecided or, if it wishes, proceed to further balloting seems to be gratuitously assumed; it certainly is not supported by the canon which does not permit more than three ballots. In an election if no candidate has obtained the requisite majority on the third ballot the presiding official may cast a deciding vote but is under no obligation to do so. This is beyond question from the obvious sense of the very text of the canon. Does every presiding official have this duty or right? Chelodi[88] thinks that only a president who is *de gremio capituli* and has the right of active suffrage can settle an equality of votes. Others say that every presiding official can do this.[89] The writer inclines to the latter opinion from a consideration of the parallel place in canon 171, § 1. In this canon when the legislator wished to impose the obligation of taking an oath only on a president who was a member of the chapter

[86] Cf. Michiels, *Principia Generalia de Personis*, p. 389 and the authors there cited in note (3).

[87] *Institutiones*, I, n. 467.

[88] *Ius de Personis*, p. 422, note (4). Cf. also Parsons, *Canonical Elections*, p. 155.

[89] E. g., Michiels, *Principia Generalia de Personis*, p. 390; Coronata, *Institutiones*, I, p. 174, note (7); Vermeersch-Crusen, *Epitome*, nn. 225, 626; Larraona, "Commentarium Codicis"—*CpR*, VIII (1927), 22; Maroto, "Annotationes"—*CpR*, XV (1934), 350, note (1).

he expressly says so.[90] So here also, if the legislator had wished that only a president who was a member of the college should settle a tie vote, he would have expressly stated this. Perhaps the only time this dispute will have a practical application in religious chapters is when the local Ordinary or religious superior is presiding in the election of a superioress for women religious. The fact that this was forbidden to the local Ordinary under pre-Code law seems to strengthen the position of those who deny him this right.[91] Nevertheless, since the Pontifical Commission for the Interpretation of the Code has declared that the local Ordinary has a true presidency of jurisdiction and not merely an honorary chairmanship,[92] it seems that it must be admitted that he has all the powers that the law confers on the president unless the contrary can be clearly proved. In the writer's opinion such a proof can come only from an authentic interpretation that the president cannot settle a tie vote according to the norm of canon 101 unless he is a voting member of the chapter.

The alternative method of settling a tie vote in elections established in this canon is that he shall be considered elected who is senior by order or by first profession or by age. Must these three norms of seniority be applied in the order here named? Some authors say that they must unless it is otherwise established by particular law.[93] The writer does not think that the legislator intended to impose the order here given as obligatory. This enumeration seems to be merely a particular application of the general norms of precedence. This view seems to be confirmed from the context, for the three words are listed disjunctively. In other words, the legislator seemingly wishes to declare elected the person who has the right of precedence. Which of the three standards is to be first applied as well as the order in which they are to be applied will be determined by the rules of precedence in the particular religious institute, for the right of precedence among the members of any college is governed

[90] ". . . cum praeside, si et ipse e gremio collegii sit . . ." Cf. also canon 397, 4°.

[91] Cf. Berutti, *De Religiosis*, n. 30, Scholion I.

[92] 30 iul. 1934—*AAS*, XXVI, 494.

[93] Vermeersch-Creusen, *Epitome*, I, n. 225; Maroto, *Institutiones*, I, p. 548, note (2); Parsons, *Canonical Elections*, pp. 153-154.

by its proper legitimate constitutions.[94] In most religious institutes precedence is governed by the first profession and there seems to be no reason why this should be abandoned.[95] Only when there are no norms for precedence in the religious institute would the order here given be obligatory.

The particular laws of the institute may establish a different norm for breaking a tie vote. The *Normae* (1901) [96] required an absolute majority even on the third ballot for the election of the Superior General. If there were no election on the third ballot, outside of Europe a fourth ballot was permitted in which only the two candidates who had the greater number of votes in the third ballot were eligible. If this resulted in a tie vote, the senior in profession was elected. Constitutions modeled on the *Normae* may be expected to contain similar provisions. Creusen remarks that many constitutions approved by the Sacred Congregations for Religious have provisions similar to this.[97]

(2) In Affairs Affecting the Capitulars as Individuals

2°. Quod autem omnes, uti singulos, tangit, ab omnibus probari debet.

When the decision to be reached will affect each one as an individual then it must be approved by all. No hard and fast rule can be given for determining when a decision is of this nature. The general rule given by authors is that actions which will take away individual rights or impose undue burdens must be approved by all.[98] Vermeersch-Creusen list as such decisions, which might occur in a religious chapter, those which would effect a reformation, impose new observances, change the form of the institute, or unite it with another religious institute.[99] It will often be very difficult to decide in a particular case whether an action is of this kind. Vermeersch-

[94] Canon 106, 5°.

[95] Coronata, *Institutiones,* I, p. 175, note (2).

[96] Art. 232-234.

[97] *Religious Men and Women in the Code,* n. 76.

[98] Coronata, *Institutiones,* I, n. 145; Maroto, *Institutiones,* I, n. 467, II.

[99] *Epitome,* n. 225.

Creusen say that in case of doubt it would be better to consult the Holy See.[100] The common law demands that decision to elect by compromise be approved by unanimous vote.[101]

It might also be asked if the decision to delegate some other business, for which the chapter is competent, must have the unanimous approval of all. The writer thinks that the solution of this question depends on whether the chapter is *exclusively* competent in the business to be delegated. If the right to decide belongs exclusively to the chapter then the decision to delegate it to others must have the unanimous approval of all, for in this case every member of the chapter has a right to have a voice in the decision and cannot be deprived of that right unless he consents. On the other hand, if the chapter has only a cumulative right and some other person or group of persons are equally competent, a majority vote would suffice, for here it would seem that all the chapter is doing is declaring that it does not wish to decide.[102] In this way the general chapter in religious institutes often decrees to leave to the Superior General and his council many things submitted to its consideration when further information is necessary or when it is foreseen that future circumstances will change the state of the question proposed.[103]

How is the expression, *ab omnibus approbari debet,* to be understood? Must the approval be expressed? It does not seem to be necessary for the validity of the action that there be express approval, but there must be solid foundation for presumption of consent. For example, if one were sufficiently notified and still absented himself, or if present did not vote, he could very justly be presumed to have renounced his right and so consented, since he could easily have ex-

[100] *Loc. cit.*

[101] Canon 172. Parsons (*Canonical Elections,* pp. 165-166) requires that this unanimous approval extend to everything set down in the written mandate of compromise. In the footnote to this section of canon 101 Cardinal Gasparri has a cross reference to canon 526. In this canon, however, only an absolute majority is required to retain the ordinary confessor beyond the three year period; the dissident, if they desire it, must be provided for in some other way.

[102] Cf. Schaefer, *De Religiosis,* p. 234; Goyeneche, "Consultationes"—*CpR,* III (1922), 222-223.

[103] Cf. Ellis, "The General Chapter of Affairs in a Religious Congregation"—*RfR,* I (1942), 256.

pressed his disapproval and did not. On the contrary, an invalid vote in itself (e.g., because uncertain or undetermined) would not be sufficient ground for such a presumption.[104] Consent extorted by force, fraud or fear will render the decision invalid or rescissible.[105]

Article V. Capitular Elections

Without doubt the most important business conducted in religious chapters is the choice of superiors who will govern the society. The present study would not, then, be complete without some discussion of this matter. On the other hand a detailed treatment of the subject would too greatly enlarge this work, so the essential points will be presented in a brief and summary form. For a fuller discussion the reader is referred to the authors who treat professedly on this topic.[106] No consideration will be given to election by acclamation, for the necessity of a secret vote rules this out for religious; nor will election by compromise be treated since it is so rarely used. The scope of the present article will, then, be confined to the essentials of election by scrutiny and of the process of postulation.

I. Election by Scrutiny

A. *The Substantial Form of Scrutiny*

Since they who violate the substantial form of election are liable to punishment to be inflicted by the Ordinary according to the gravity of the fault.[107] it will be well to determine first of all what are the formalities or solemnities which constitute the substantial form of election by scrutiny. Maroto [108] proposes two criteria for determining what are the formalities which pertain to the substantial form of election: (a) those to which an invalidating sanction has been at-

[104] Cf. Coronata, *Institutiones,* I, n. 145.

[105] Canon 103.

[106] Perhaps the most complete work in English on the subject is the dissertation of Rev. Anscar Parsons, O.M.Cap., *Canonical Elections,* frequently cited in this study.

[107] Canon 2391, § 2.

[108] *Institutiones,* I, n. 660, III.

tached; (b) those without which the form of election would cease to exist. Applying these criteria to the form of scrutiny he determines that the following pertain to its substance: (1) there must be tellers or scrutineers; (2) at least two, or one with the president, for they are to testify to the election and for juridic proof at least two witnesses are required; (3) the votes must be cast with some intervention of the tellers; (4) the tellers must count, examine and determine the result of the votes; (5) they must make public the result.[109] Hence all other formalities will be only accidental; e. g., that the tellers be elected, take the oath, that the votes be collected in some determined way, etc. No penalty is established in the law for violators of the substantial form, but it is left to the judgment of the Ordinary to punish them according to the gravity of their fault.

B. *The Requisites for a Valid Vote.*

1. On the part of the person voting. In order to cast a valid vote one must have the qualifications demanded by law for the right of suffrage,[110] be capable of voting,[111] and present at the chapter unless a vote by letter or proxy is admitted by particular law.[112]

2. On the part of the vote itself:

Canon 169: § 1. Suffragium est nullum, nisi fuerit:

1° Liberum; et ideo invalidum est suffragium, si elector metu gravi aut dolo, directe vel indirecte, adactus fuerit ad eligendam certam personam aut plures disiunctive;

2° Secretum, certum, absolutum, determinatum.

§ 2. Conditiones ante electionem suffragio appositae tanquam non adiectae censentur.

[109] *Op. cit.*, n. 660, IV.

[110] One who lacks these qualifications is the *extraneus* of canon 165. Cf. Parsons, *Canonical Elections*, pp. 115-120. If such a person is willingly admitted by the chapter the election is invalid, but if he participates without the knowledge and consent of the chapter only the vote will be invalid.

[111] He should not be one prevented from voting as in canon 167. This canon has already been discussed, cf. Chapter VI, Article II, II, B.

[112] Canon 163. Cf. Article I, C, of this chapter.

Canon 170: Suffragium sibimetipsi nemo valide dare potest.

(a) *Free.* As the canon states a vote is invalid if it is extorted directly or indirectly by grave fear or fraud; that is, if the voter in order to free himself from the fear is forced to choose a certain person or several persons disjunctively proposed to him, or by fraud is tricked into this. Physical force is not mentioned here because actions of persons performed under such force are always invalid.[113] All who impede this liberty of choice in any way or who, after the completion of the election, molest the electors or the elected are to be punished in proportion to the gravity of their fault. If the freedom of election is impeded because of the interference of the secular or lay power, all the electors who solicited this interference or willingly assented to it are, *ipso facto,* deprived of their right of electing for that time; one who knowingly consents to his own election made under these conditions becomes, *ipso facto,* unqualified for the office or benefice.[114]

(b) *Secret.* A vote ceases to be secret when the name of the elected and the elector becomes publicly known in the actual process of voting. Thus it would not be an invalid vote if the elector informed one or two other electors for whom he was voting; [115] likewise, it would not be invalid if the voter manifested before or after the election the person of his choice.[116]

(c) *Certain.* A vote is certain if the person voted for can be known without any fear of error. A vote for Caius, when it could apply to several of that name, would be uncertain and invalid. If the writing could not be deciphered or the sense understood it would also be an uncertain vote and, consequently, invalid.[117]

(d) *Absolute.* The vote must not be conditioned. This applies only to conditions expressed in the vote itself, since according to § 2 of canon 169 conditions placed beforehand have no effect. A condi-

[113] Canon 103, § 1.
[114] Canon 2390, §§ 1-2.
[115] Cf. Schaefer, *De Religiosis,* p. 270.
[116] Maroto, *Institutiones,* I, n. 624, II.
[117] Maroto, *loc. cit.*

tion to invalidate the vote must be extrinsic to it, for conditions intrinsic to it are always understood; hence, expressing them would serve no purpose but it would not invalidate the vote, e. g., I elect Caius if he is eligible.

(e) *Determined.* It is very difficult to draw an exact dividing line between a certain vote and a determined vote, but it is not necessary to do so since both are required. Thus an alternative vote, for Peter or Paul, would not be determined nor would it be certain. A vote showing an undecided will would be undetermined, e. g., I would wish to elect Caius.[118] In the case of an uncertain or indeterminate vote the elector could be approached by the scrutineers and asked to explain his vote or cast a new vote.[119]

(f) *Not cast for oneself.* This needs no explanation.

(g) *Cast for an eligible candidate.* It is quite clear that a vote cast for one who is not eligible is of no avail.

(h) *One from each voter.* The excess of votes by one who attempts to cast more than one vote in his own name will be invalid.[120]

An invalid vote or votes, *in se,* do not invalidate the election. They will do this, however, in two cases: (a) if the person elected would not have the requisite majority without the invalid votes; (b) if one who was laboring under excommunication inflicted by declaratory or condemnatory sentence was knowingly admitted to vote.[121]

C. *The Manner of Voting*

The choice of the electors, from the very nature of things, must be manifested by some external sign, otherwise it could not be known. No definite manner of voting is prescribed in the common law for elections in general or for religious elections in particular. The ordinary way is by a written vote and this seems to be supposed in the general law of elections; but other ways are not excluded.[122] Canon 168 prescribes that the tellers obtain a written vote from an elector

[118] Coronata, *Institutiones,* I, n. 238.

[119] Coronata, *loc. cit.*

[120] Canon 164. Cf. Article I, E, of this chapter.

[121] Canon 167, § 2.

[122] Maroto, *Institutiones,* I, n. 634.

who is ill,[123] but authors say that if such a person cannot write he may manifest his choice orally to the tellers and they will write it down.[124] There is certainly no obligation to use a form of written vote on which the elector's name or a distinguishing sign is written, as is done in the election of the Pope, for this form of vote is not even suggested in the general laws on elections. The prescriptions concerning the manner of voting and the form of the written vote will have to be determined by the particular law or the accepted practice of each religious institute.

D. *The Collecting of the Votes*

Canon 171: § 2. Scrutatores curent ut suffragia secreto, diligenter, singillatim et servato praecedentiae ordine ab unoquoque electore ferantur. . . .

The intervention of tellers or scrutineers in the actual collection of the votes is necessary for the validity of an election by scrutiny.[125] The law prescribes that at least two be appointed [126] but one together with the president of the chapter will be sufficient for the validity of the election.[127] The president and the tellers ought to sit apart from the other electors where they can be seen but not heard in examining the votes if they be written or in receiving them if they are communicated orally. It is the duty of the tellers to see to it that the votes are cast by each elector:

(a) *Secretly.* That is to say that the vote, if it be written, is folded or sealed in such a way that no one can see for whom the vote is cast; or if it be oral, that it is not communicated in a tone of voice loud enough to be heard by the other electors.

(b) *Diligently.* Authors seem to experience difficulty in explaining the meaning of this term. In the opinion of the present writer, authors who interpret the word as determining the manner in which

[123] " . . . suffragium eius scriptum a scrutatoribus exquiratur. . . ."

[124] E. g., Parsons, *Canonical Elections,* p. 114.

[125] Coronata, *Institutiones,* I, n. 235; Maroto, *Institutiones,* I, n. 660.

[126] Canon 171, § 1.

[127] Maroto, *loc. cit.;* Coronata, *op. cit.,* n. 234.

the tellers should fulfill their duty seem to disregard the grammatical construction of the canon. Certainly no one will question the assertion that the tellers should be diligent in the performance of their duty, but that is not prescribed by this canon. What the canon does say is that the tellers shall see to it that the suffrages are cast diligently by the electors; that is, the tellers have an obligation to see that diligence is used by the electors in the actual physical process of voting. Hence the writer believes that Leitner [128] is much closer to the true meaning of *diligenter,* as used here, when he interprets it as without loss of time and with a careful handling of the ballot,[129] than are the authors who interpret it to mean that the tellers should perform their duty carefully,[130] or should be vigilant lest any voter cast more than one vote or extract any vote already cast,[131] or should examine well and carefully note down each vote.[132]

(c) *Singly.* The voters should approach the tellers or be approached by them singly, and not in twos or threes or in a crowd for this would endanger the secrecy of the vote.

(d) *In the order of precedence.* First the president, then the tellers, and then the other electors in the order of precedence established by the accepted practice of each chapter.

A violation of any of these prescriptions concerning the manner of casting a vote, except the one demanding secrecy, will have no effect on the validity of the vote.

Since the priest tellers in the election of the superioress of a community of nuns may not enter the cloister, it is impossible for them to obtain the vote of a nun who is sick. In this case the president should appoint two of the nuns to act as tellers to obtain the vote. Since these nuns would be *e gremio capituli* it seems that they should take the oath prescribed by canon 171 § 1.

[128] Cited by Schaefer, *De Religiosis,* p. 280, note (302).

[129] Cf. also Aloisius a S. Francisco Paulano, *De Capitulis,* p. 119.

[130] Parsons, *Canonical Elections,* p. 150.

[131] Coronata, *Institutiones,* I, n. 235; Maroto, *Institutiones,* I, n. 634.

[132] Vermeersch-Creusen, *Epitome,* I, n. 287; Wernz-Vidal, *Ius Canonicum,* II, n. 257.

E. *The Counting, the Reading, and the Announcing of the Votes*

Canon 171: § 2. . . . collectisque ad ultimum suffragiis, coram praeside electionis, secundum formam propriis constitutionibus vel legitimis consuetudinibus statutam, inspiciant an suffragiorum numerus respondeat numero electorum, suffragia ipsa scrutentur palamque faciant quot quisque retulerit.

§ 3. Si numerus suffragiorum superet numerum eligentium, nihil est actum.

After the votes have all been collected, they should be counted to determine whether or not the ballot is valid according to the norm given above in treating of capitular decisions in general.[133] If the ballot is found to be valid the tellers proceed to read and announce the votes.

The reading and announcing of the results of the voting are required for validity in this form of election.[134] No particular manner of doing this is prescribed. If the votes are written two ways are possible. The president will open each vote, read it and pass it to the first teller who will read it and note it down, then he will pass it to the second teller who will do the same. After all have been read and noted down, the result of the balloting will be announced. The other way is that the second teller will announce each vote after he reads it. Since the canon prescribes that it must be announced how many votes each candidate received, any contrary practice must be considered as abrogated.[135] It does not seem to be required for the validity of the election that it be announced how many votes each candidate received, for an invalidating sanction is not expressly stated nor does this seem to be a formality without which this form of election would cease to exist.[136] In the opinion of the writer, Creusen is unduly concerned about the violation of the secrecy of the vote which may occur in carrying out the prescription of the law in this matter. He says:

[133] Article IV, C.

[134] Coronata, *Institutiones,* I, n. 237.

[135] Coronata, *loc. cit.*

[136] Coronata, *loc. cit.*

> ". . . when a superior general is elected unanimously, with his own vote excepted, his vote by the very nature of things becomes public, a thing absolutely prohibited by the Code. Seemingly, the only way to avoid this inconvenience would be not to announce the votes as soon as they are opened, but only after having examined the entire scrutiny, and not to announce the single vote, the author of which would thus be betrayed." [137]

He seems to have overlooked the fact that there would be the same violation of secrecy every time the votes were divided between two voting members of the chapter, for the presumption would be that each voted for the other. If the votes were equally divided, should the names of both candidates be suppressed to avoid the violation of secrecy? That, surely, would be absurd. In the opinion of the writer such violations of secrecy are unavoilably connected with the carrying out of the prescriptions of the law and so need not be cause for concern. It certainly would not be reasonable to consider a vote invalid because it was revealed in this way.

F. *The Determining and the Proclamation of the Election*

Canon 174: Is electus habeatur et a collegii praeside proclametur, qui requisitum suffragiorum numerum retulerit, ad normam can. 101, § 1, n. 1.

The result of the election is to be determined according to the norms that have already been given in treating of capitular decisions in general.[138] When any candidate has received the necessary majority the presiding official formally proclaims his election. Formerly this was an essential part of a canonical election, but at present the omission of it would have no effect on the validity of the election.[139] The canon says that the president should proclaim the election, but he may appoint another to do this.[140] It is probable that a contrary custom according to which one of the tellers proclaimed the election

[137] *Religious Men and Women in the Code,* n. 76.

[138] Article IV, D.

[139] Coronata, *Institutiones,* I, n. 248.

[140] "Potest quis per alium, quod potest facere per seipsum."—Reg. 68, R. J. in VI°.

could still be followed.[141] The precise formula of this decree of election, if there be one, can be ascertained only by investigating the accepted practice or particular law of each institute.[142]

G. *The Burning of the Votes*

Canon 171: § 4. Suffragia statim, peracto unoquoque scrutinio, vel post sessionem, si in eadem sessione habeantur plura scrutinia, comburantur.

After each ballot, or after each session if more than one ballot were taken during the session, the votes should be burned. There seems to be no obligation to burn the votes if they contain only the name of the person voted for and not also the name of the elector, since this prescription is directed toward the protection of the secrecy of the vote, particularly to prevent it becoming known for whom an individual elector voted.[143]

H. *The Notification and the Refusal or Acceptance of the Election*

1. Notification of the Person Elected

Canon 175: Electio illico intimanda est electo, qui debet saltem intra octiduum utile a recepta intimatione manifestare utrum electioni consentiat, an eidem renuntiet; secus omne ius ex electione quaesitum amittit.

Once some person has received the necessary majority and the president has officially proclaimed the election, the law demands that the person elected be immediately notified of his election. The burden of notifying the person elected rests on the whole electoral body, but principally on the president for the whole reason of his office is to see that all the prescriptions of law are carried out.[144] Clearly if the person elected is present at the voting there is no need for a formal notification because he already knows of his election

141 Coronata, *loc. cit.*

142 Cf. Aloisius a S. Francisco Paulano, *De Capitulis,* p. 171.

143 *Idem.,* p. 129.

144 Maroto, *Institutiones,* I, n. 667.

from the formal announcement. No special manner (e. g., personal notification, letter, telephone, telegraph) is prescribed and so, unless there is some manner prescribed by particular law, any method of making the notification may be used. The quickest way would seem to be the best way, for until the one elected has signified his acceptance or refusal the process of filling the office is at a standstill. This view is supported by the provision in the pre-Code law that the elected was to be notified as quickly as possible.[145] The law does not specify any period of time within which notification must be made. Delay, however, is of no advantage to the electors and may result in the loss of their right to elect if the election is not completed with the time specified by law.[146]

The person elected has eight days in which to decide whether he will accept or reject the election. The time begins to elapse from midnight of the day the notice was received since the *terminus a quo* does not coincide with the beginning of a day.[147] It is *tempus utile* and hence will not elapse when he is hindered from acting.[148] It is sufficient that he dispatch his reply before the time permitted him by law has elapsed and it is not required that it reach the chapter within that time. If the elected person fails to comply with this prescription he loses the right he acquired by the election. This is merely a right that no other be elected during the time permitted for deliberation and not a right to the office, either *ad rem* or *in re,* for this is acquired either by acceptance or by acceptance and confirmation.[149]

2. Refusal of the Election

Canon 176: § 1. Si electus renuntiaverit, omne ius ex electione quaesitum amittit, etsi renuntiationis eum postea poeniteat; sed rursus eligi potest; collegium autem intra mensem a cognita renuntiatione ad novam electionem procedere debet.

[145] ". . . quam citius commode potest"—c. 6, *de electione et electi potestate,* I, 6, in VI°.

[146] Canon 161.

[147] Canon 34, § 3, 3°.

[148] Canon 35.

[149] Canon 176, § 2.

A renunciation of the election takes away the right acquired by the election, even if the elected person afterwards regrets the fact that he refused. It does not, however, render him in any way disqualified for the office and he may again be elected, as the canon clearly states. The refusal may be tacit or expressed. The only tacit refusal that may be acted on is a failure to manifest acceptance within the time prescribed by law. During the time prescribed for deliberation the chapter cannot proceed to a new election unless the person elected has expressly refused to accept. For example, if the person elected merely expressed an unwillingness to accept, this could not be considered as a renunciation of the election.[150] If the elected person renounces the election or fails to reply, the chapter must proceed to a new election within a month.

It has been and still is a disputed question whether a religious who has been elected to an office in his society can renounce the election and whether acceptance can be imposed by the precept of a legitimate superior. Certainly if the Rules and Constitutions prohibit renunciation the question is settled and the religious must accept and can even be forced to accept by a precept obliging under the vow of obedience, since the constitutions are the remote matter of this vow. It is equally certain that if the constitutions expressly permit renunciation the religious is free to accept or reject the election and no superior can compel acceptance since the power of a superior is circumscribed by the constitutions. What is the solution when the constitutions are silent? Larraona [151] says that the opinion which affirms the juridic obligation of accepting is supported by the cogency of the reasons it adduces and the authority of the authors who propose it, is confirmed by the law and practice of most religious institutes, both ancient and modern, and is consequently more probable. Nevertheless, the present writer inclines to the contrary opinion favoring the liberty of the religious to accept or refuse. A certain obligation can arise only from a certain source. Where is the certain source of this obligation? Clearly not from the common law, for canon 175 permits anyone to renounce an election and nowhere does it deny this liberty

[150] Maroto, *Institutiones,* I, n. 649.
[151] "Consultationes"—*CpR,* II (1921), 340-342.

to religious. In like manner the particular law cannot be the source of this obligation, for this case is proposed on the supposition that there are no prescriptions of particular law which impose this obligation. Since, then, the obligation is imposed by neither common nor particular law, it does not seem to exist.[152] The further question remains, when such prescriptions of particular law are lacking can the superior impose a precept compelling one to accept the election? On this point the writer is inclined to agree with Augustine when he says: "Hence not even the superior can compel a religious to accept an election, because the freedom to refuse office has not been taken away by profession."[153] The religious is obliged to obey only according to the constitutions and in the present case there is no pertinent prescription in the constitutions. It is true that it is implicitly contained in all constitutions that the superior can command whatever is for the common good of the institute, but it seems to be stretching a point to make the common good of the society depend on the acceptance of office by an individual religious. If the same religious were to seek office because it was for the common good of the society that he be elected, he would be considered as totally lacking in religious humility. The objection that if all the members of the order were to refuse office it would be contrary to the common good of the institute is unquestionably true but hardly valid as an argument. Like the similar objection that would impose on every human individual an obligation to marry, it is founded upon a hypothesis which, considering the nature of man, lacks even remote possibility of ever being verified. In practice, if such a precept is imposed, the religious should obey and then have recourse to the proper superior to have the precept rescinded.[154]

[152] Cf. Ellis, "The General Chapter of Elections in a Religious Congregation"—*RfR,* I (1942), 153; Vermeersch, "Quaesita Propria Religiosorum," 10—*Periodica de Re Canonica et Morali utili praesertim Religiosis et Missionariis* (Brugis, 1905—), XI (1923), 153; Fanfani, *De Iure Religiosorum,* n. 107.

[153] *A Commentary,* II, 144-145.

[154] It should be remembered that the above is a juridic and not an ascetic discussion. The solution of the question whether it would be the better thing and that which is more in conformity with the religious spirit, to accept an office to which one has been elected is left to the writers on the spiritual life and ascetical theology.

3. Acceptance of the Election

Canon 176: § 2. Acceptatione electionis electus, si confirmatione non egeat, plenum ius statim obtinet; secus, non acquirit nisi ius ad rem.

Acceptance of the election confers on the person elected a strict right to the office. If the election needs confirmation, he obtains only a *ius ad rem,* that is, he has a right to be confirmed and this can be denied only for a legitimate reason. If the election does not need confirmation, he immediately obtains a *ius in re,* the full right to the office itself, and can begin to exercise it at once, unless some form of corporal installation is required. The acceptance of the office should be expressed, but it could be implicit, e. g., if the person elected accepted the obedience of the voters, made the profession of faith, petitioned confirmation, or clearly revealed his acceptance of the election in other ways. The acceptance of the election finishes the process of filling the office on the part of the religious chapter. The confirmation of the election will be treated in the succeeding chapter.

II. Postulation

A. *The Concept of Postulation and Its Use in Religious Chapters*

Postulation, as it is described in canon 179, § 1, is the act by which the electors by their suffrage propose to a competent superior a candidate, whom they consider most fit but whom they cannot elect because of an impediment from which the superior can and usually is willing to dispense. The common law permits postulation for any office unless it is otherwise provided by law. They, however, who have the right of election by reason of a compromise cannot proceed by postulation unless this is expressed in the document committing the election to them.[155] The law does not favor postulation in religious chapters and permits it only in extraordinary cases, but, even then, not if it is forbidden by the constitutions.[156] The admis-

[155] Canon 179, § 2.

[156] "Postulatio admitti potest solum in casu extraordinario et dummodo in constitutionibus non prohibeatur"—canon 507, § 3.

sion of postulation by a competent superior means that he concedes a dispensation from some law. Therefore, the electors in submitting a postulation to this superior must also submit a just and reasonable cause proportionate to the gravity of the law from which the dispensation is asked; without such a cause the dispensation, and consequently the postulation, conceded by one inferior to the legislator is illicit and invalid.[157] The members of a religious chapter should keep in mind that the Sacred Congregation for Religious has declared that the simple desire of the voters or the fitness of the person is not a sufficient reason for the dispensation.[158]

B. *The Form of Postulation*

Postulation, like election, is accomplished by the suffrage of the electors. In order to postulate validly the elector must make use of the formula, "I postulate" or some equivalent formula.[159] If the elector is doubtful whether the impediment exists he may use the formula "I elect or I postulate" and then his vote will be valid for election if the impediment does not exist or for postulation if the impediment is really present.[160]

For a valid postulation the candidate must always have at least an absolute majority of the votes cast.[161] Hence a candidate will never be validly postulated by a relative majority even on the third ballot. Moreover, if in the balloting eligible candidates are also being voted for, the postulated will have to obtain two thirds of the votes.[162] On the third ballot in which postulation concurs with election, if the postulated candidate does not have the requisite two thirds of the votes, the elegible candidate who has a relative majority over any other eligible candidate is elected.[163] An example will

[157] Canon 84.

[158] 9 mar. 1920—*AAS*, 365.

[159] Canon 180, § 2.

[160] Canon 180, § 2.

[161] Canon 180, § 1.

[162] Canon 180, § 1.

[163] Cf. Pont. Com. Interp., I iul. 1922—*AAS*, XXIV, 406.

illustrate this. Twenty one valid votes are cast. The postulated candidate obtains thirteen votes, one eligible candidate obtains five, and another eligible candidate obtains three; the eligible candidate with five votes is elected. If the two eligible candidates obtained four votes each, then the parity of votes would be broken according to the norm given above,[164] the postulated candidate being always excluded.

C. *The Competent Superior*

Within eight days the postulation must be sent to a competent superior.[165] This superior will have to be one who has the faculty to dispense from the impediment. Hence if the incapacity arises from an impediment established in the Code, the competent superior will be the Sacred Congregation for Religious. If the impediment is established by the constitutions the competent superior will be one capable of dispensing from them. If the superior who has the right to confirm the election is competent to concede the dispensation the postulation must be sent to him.[166]

D. *Effects of Postulation*

(a) Before the assent to the postulation by the competent superior. By postulation the one postulated acquires no right to the office and it is lawful for the superior to reject it. No reason seems to be needed for this rejection. Once the postulation has been presented to the superior the electors cannot recall it unless the superior consents.[167]

(b) After the assent to the postulation by the competent superior. If the superior admits the postulation then the one postulated should be notified. Eight days are permitted the postulated candidate in which to deliberate whether he will accept. If he refuses the office or if he does not manifest his acceptance within the prescribed time,

[164] Article IV, C.

[165] Canon 181, § 1. This is *tempus utile* as can be seen from the concluding clause of § 2 of this canon: ". . . nisi probent se a mittenda postulatione iusto detentos fuisse impedimento."

[166] Canon 181, § 1.

[167] Canon 181, §§ 3-4.

the right of election returns to the chapter.[168] If he accepts, he immediately acquires full right to the office.[169]

(c) After rejection of the postulation by the competent superior. If the superior rejects the postulation the right of election returns to the chapter.[170]

E. *Defects in Postulation and Consequent Penalties*

If the postulation is not sent within eight days and the electors cannot prove that they were reasonably hindered from sending it, the electors are deprived of the right of electing or postulating for this instance. The right of provision for the office in question will devolve upon the superior who has the right to confirm the election, or if the election does not need confirmation, to the superior to whom the right of filling the office successively belongs.[171]

If the electors knowingly postulate one who is hindered from being elected by an impediment which cannot be dispensed or from which the superior will not ordinarily dispense, they are deprived of the right of electing or postulating for that time and the provision of an appointee for the office will devolve upon the superior. This superior will be determined in the same manner as in the preceding penalty.[172]

Article VI. The Conclusion of the Celebration of the Religious Chapter

The celebration of the chapter is concluded by the reading and signing of the acts of the chapter. The common law prescribes that all the acts of the elections be taken down by the secretary. These acts are to be signed by the secretary, the president and the tellers.[173]

[168] Canon 182, § 2. This time is to be reckoned in the same manner as the eight days for the acceptance of election.

[169] Canon 182, § 3.

[170] Canon 182, § 1.

[171] Canons 182, § 2; 178.

[172] Canon 182, § 1.

[173] Canon 171, § 5.

It is the usual practice that the secretary write down all the acts of the chapter. Sometimes all the capitulars sign the acts.[174] The acts of the chapter are to be preserved in the archives.[175] After the acts have been read and signed the chapter is adjourned.

[174] E. g., in the provincial and general chapter among the Passionists, cf. Aloisius a S. Francisco Paulano, *De Capitulis,* p. 129. Cf. also Ellis, "The General Chapter of Affairs in a Religious Congregation"—*RfR,* I (1942), p. 258.

[175] Canon 171, § 5.

CHAPTER VIII

THE CONFIRMATION OF THE RELIGIOUS CHAPTER

A. *The Nature of Confirmation*

CONFIRMATION may be described as the act by which a competent superior approves the acts of the chapter and by this approval renders them firm.[1] In an election it is the final act in the process of filling the office and by it the office is actually conferred.[2]

B. *The Necessity of Confirmation*

In general it may be said that the acts of moral persons are concluded by the votes of those who have the right of suffrage.[3] Sometimes, however, the law prescribes that the acts be submitted to a superior for confirmation. Ordinarily confirmation seems to be required for election. This can be deduced from the canon treating of the ways of canonical provision of appointees for office.[4] The canon says that provision of appointees for office is made by confirmation if election preceded or by election and acceptance if the election does not need confirmation. This seems to say that the election which does not need confirmation is the exception. Even for election, however, confirmation does not seem to be necessary unless it is expressly prescribed. In general, then, it seems that it may be said that acts of a religious chapter do not need confirmation unless it is expressly prescribed. There is no prescription of common law that requires that the acts of religious chapters be confirmed. The only definite prescription of the Code touching this matter is canon 506, § 4 which recognizes the right of the local ordinary to confirm

[1] Cf. Aloisius a S. Francisco Paulano, *De Capitulis*, pp. 145-146.

[2] Cf. Coronata, *Institutiones*, I, n. 251.

[3] Maroto, *Institutiones*, I, n. 468, V.

[4] Canon 148, § 1.

or rescind the election of the Superioress General of a diocesan congregation. Authors say that the Holy See usually requires that the acts of general chapters of more recent pontifical congregations be submitted to itself for approval.[5] There is no general precept to this effect and unless the constitutions require such confirmation, the acts need not be submitted to the Holy See.[6] The local Ordinary may reserve to himself the right to confirm the acts of the chapter of affairs in a diocesan congregation; if he has not done so, there is no obligation to submit the acts to him for approval.[7] This is about all that can be said concerning the confirmation of the acts of religious chapters generally considered. Further and more definite prescriptions concerning this confirmation must be discovered from the particular laws of each institute. The rest of this chapter will be concerned with the confirmation of elections.

C. *The Competent Superior for Confirmation*

In only one case is the superior competent to confirm an election in a religious chapter determined by the Code. The local Ordinary who presides at the election of the Superioress General in a congregation of diocesan approval has the right to confirm or rescind the election.[8] Unless it is otherwise provided by particular law, ordinarily the competent superior is the immediate ecclesiastical superior of the office and the person elected.[9] Very frequently the supreme superiors in pontifical institutes are considered as confirmed by the Holy See by the fact of election.[10] Sometimes other superiors are confirmed in the same way.[11]

[5] E. g., Coronata, *Institutiones*, I, n. 535.

[6] Ellis, "The General Chapter of Affairs in a Religious Congregation"—*RfR*, I (1942), 258.

[7] Ellis, *loc. cit.*

[8] Canon 506, § 4.

[9] Maroto, *Institutiones*, I, n. 651, (B).

[10] Wernz-Vidal, *Ius Canonicum*, II, n. 266.

[11] E. g., the general councilors and the provincial superior and his councilors among the Passionists. Cf. Aloisius a S. Francisco Paulano, *De Capitulis*, pp. 146-148.

D. *The Petition for Confirmation*

Canon 177: § 1. Electus, si electio confirmatione indigeat, saltem intra octiduum a die acceptatae electionis confirmationem a competente Superiore petere per se vel per alium debet; secus omni iure privatur, nisi probaverit se a petenda confirmatione iusto impedimento fuisse detentum.

The petition for confirmation of the election, when it is required, must be directed to the competent superior within eight days from the time the election was accepted, otherwise all right acquired by the person elected is lost. This is *tempus utile* as is clearly shown by the clause that if a just impediment prevents action the acquired right is not lost. The lapse of time is to be reckoned according to the norm of canon 34, 3°. The obligation to petition for confirmation rests principally upon the person elected, but he may make his petition through another. The chapter could petition for the confirmation by sending the acts of the chapter to the competent superior.[12]

E. *The Judgment Involved in Confirmation*

Canon 177: § 2. Superior, si electum repererit idoneum, et electio ad normam iuris fuerit peracta, nequit confirmationem denegare.

The superior is not absolutely free in regard to confirming the election, for if, after he has made his investigation, he finds that the candidate is fit and the election validly performed, he cannot deny confirmation. No special way of making an investigation into the legality of the election and the fitness of the candidate is prescribed, so the superior may make it in the way that seems best to him. If the acts of the chapter are submitted to him and he finds that everything was performed legitimately, he may base his judgment upon these and confirm the election.[13]

[12] Parsons, *Canonical Elections*, p. 181.

[13] Coronata, *Institutiones*, I, 251.

F. *The Time and Manner of Confirmation*

Canon 177: § 3. Confirmatio in scriptis dari debet.

No definite time is prescribed within which the superior must confirm the election. If the chapter or the person elected feels that the superior is delaying the confirmation unreasonably, recourse may be had to a competent superior either to confirm the election or compel the negligent superior to act.[14] In regard to the manner, the common law prescribes only that the confirmation be given in writing; particular law may determine the manner more definitely and would then have to be observed.[15]

G. *The Effects of Confirmation*

1. If the confirmation is conceded. By confirmation of the election the canonical process of provision is completed and the person elected may enter upon the exercise of the office unless some further formality is prescribed, e. g., corporal installation or blessing.

2. If the confirmation is denied. The effects following upon denial of confirmation vary depending upon the reason why the confirmation was denied.

(a) If the superior refuses to confirm because of some defect which deprives the whole chapter of the right of election, the right of provision of an appointee for the office devolves upon this superior.[16] These defects are: (1) failure to complete the election within the prescribed time;[17] (2) soliciting or spontaneously admitting the interference of the secular power in the election;[18] (3) *deliberately* electing an unworthy person;[19] (4) committing the crime of simony in the election;[20] (5) presuming to actually confer the office, neglecting the authority of the superior who has a right to confirm the election;[21]

[14] Parsons, *Canonical Elections*, p. 185.
[15] Maroto, *Institutiones*, I, p. 776, note (1).
[16] Canon 178.
[17] Canons 161, 178.
[18] Canon 2390, § 2.
[19] Canon 2391, § 1.
[20] Canon 2392, 2°.
[21] Canon 2393.

(6) and admitting someone to office before presentation of his letters of confirmation.[22]

(b) If the superior refused confirmation because *some* of the electors were guilty of the crimes from (2) to (6) above, the right to elect returns to the innocent.[23] In like manner if the superior refused to confirm the election for some reason which did not deprive the electors of their right to elect, the chapter could proceed to a new election, unless the constitutions decree that in every case of denial of confirmation the right to provide devolves upon the superior.[24] Since no time is established within which the chapter should proceed to a new election, a month may be permitted by analogy; for this is the time permitted after renunciation of election and rejection of postulation.[25]

(c) If the person elected thinks the confirmation was unjustly denied he may have recourse to a competent superior to remedy the injustice for he has a strict right to confirmation. Every right is protected by a legal action.[26]

[22] Canon 2394, 3°.
[23] Maroto, *Institutiones,* I, p. 776, note (2).
[24] Cf. Maroto, *loc. cit.,* note (3).
[25] Cf. canons 20, 176; Maroto, *op. cit.,* n. 651, (H).
[26] Canon 1667.

CONCLUSIONS

THE following are some of the more particular positive conclusions that have been reached in the course of the preceding study.

1. The religious chapter is a collegiate moral person, at least representatively, and must, therefore, abide by the laws governing the collegiate actions of such persons.

2. The religious chapter cannot deprive of his office a superior whom it has elected.

3. Unless the particular law provides otherwise, the superior competent to convoke a religious chapter is the superior of the moral person represented by the chapter, and not necessarily the person who will preside at the actual celebration of the chapter.

4. The right of active suffrage, in itself, does not impose on the religious possessing it an obligation to take part in the chapter.

5. Every presiding official, even if he is not a voting member of the chapter, has the duty or right, conveyed by canon 101, to settle a parity of votes on the third ballot, unless the contrary can be clearly proved.

6. The decision to delegate to others the solution of business for which the chapter is exclusively competent must be approved by a unanimous vote.

7. Election to an office in the religious institute, in itself, does not impose on the religious elected an obligation to accept the election.

BIBLIOGRAPHY

SOURCES

Acta Apostolicae Sedis, Commentarium Officiale, Romae, 1909—

Bouscaren, T. Lincoln, *Canon Law Digest,* 2 vols. and Supplement, Milwaukee: Bruce, 1934, 1937; Suppl., 1941.

Bullarum Diplomatum et Privilegiorum Sanctorum Romanorum Pontificum, Taurinensis Editio, Auspicante Cardinali Francisco Gaude, 25 vols., Augustae Taurinorum, 1857-1872.

Bullarium Ordinis Fratrum Minorum Capucinorum, ed. a Michaele a Tugio in Helvetia, 7 vols., Romae, 1740-1752.

Canones et Decreta Sacrosancti Oecumenici Concilii Tridentini, Editio novissima ad fidem optimorum exemplarium castigate impressa, Taurini, 1913.

Codex Iuris Canonici Pii X Pontificis Maximi iussu digestus, Benedictus XV auctoritate promulgatus, Romae: Typis Polyglottis Vaticanis, 1917.

Codicis Iuris Canonici Fontes cura Emi. Petri Card. Gasparri editi, 9 vols., Romae (later Civitate Vaticana): Typis Polyglottis Vaticanis, 1923-1939 (vols. VII, VIII, IX ed. cura et studio Emi. Iustiniani Card. Seredi).

Collectanea in Usum Secretariae Sacrae Congregationis Episcoporum et Regularium, ed. A. Bizzarri, Romae, 1885.

Corpus Iuris Canonici, Editio Lipsiensis II post Aemelii Ludovici Richteri curas instruxit Aemilius Friedberg, 1879-1881. Editio anastatice repetita, Lipsiae: Tauchnitz, 1922.

Corpus Iuris Civilis (Kreuger-Mommsen-Schoell-Kroll), 3 vols., Berolini, 1928-1929.

Declarations on the Holy Rule and Constitutions of the Swiss-American Congregation, O.S.B., translated from the Latin original as approved by the Sacred Congregation for Religious, September 9, 1924, Conception Abbey, Conception, Mo.: Altar and Home Press, 1938.

Die Constitutionen des Predigerordens in der Redaction Raimunds von Peñafort, ed. Heinrich Denifle—*Archiv für Literatur-und Kirchengeschichte des Mittelalters,* Vol. V, Freiburg im Breisgau, 1899.

Die Constitutionen des Prediger-Ordens vom Jahre 1228, ed. Heinrich Denifle—*Archiv für Literatur-und Kirchengeschichte des Mittelalters,* Vol. I, Berlin, 1885.

Haddan, A. W., and Stubbs, W., *Councils and Ecclesiastical Documents Relating to Great Britain and Ireland,* 3 vols., Oxford, 1869-1873.

Hardouin, Jean, *Acta Conciliorum et Epistolae Decretales ac Constitutiones Summorum Pontificum,* 12 vols., Parisiis, 1715.

Jaffé, Phillipus, *Regesta Pontificum Romanorum ab Condita Ecclesia ad Annum post Christum Natum MCXCVIII*, 2. ed., correctam et auctam auspiciis Gulielmi Wattenbach, curaverunt S. Loewenfeld, F. Kaltenbrunner, P. Ewald, 2 vols. in 1, Lipsiae, 1885-1888.

Mansi, J. D., *Sacrorum Conciliorum Nova et Amplissima Collectio*, 53 vols. in 59, Paris, Arnhem, Leipzig, 1901-1927.

Migne, P. J., *Patrologiae Cursus Completus—Series Latina (MPL)*, 221 vols., Parisiis, 1844-1855;—*Series Graeca (MPG)*, 161 vols., Parisiis, 1857-1866.

Monasticon Anglicanum, William Dugdale, 2. ed., Calley-Ellis-Bandinel, 6 vols. in 8, London, 1817-1830.

Monumenta Germaniae Historica (MGH), Leges, 5 vols., I-IV, ed. Pertz; V, ed. Pertz-Waitz-Brunner, Hannoverae, 1835-1889.

Normae secundum quas Sacra Congregatio Episcoporum et Regularium in novis religiosis congregationibus approbandis procedere solet, Romae, 1901.

Potthast, Augustus, *Regesta Pontificum Romanorum inde ab anno post Christum Natum MCXCVIII ad annum MCCCIV*, 2 vols., Berolini, 1874-1875.

Sancti Benedicti Regula Monasteriorum, Editio Critico-Practica, ed. Dom Cuthbert Butler, 2. ed., Friburgi Brisgoviae: Herder, 1927.

Schroeder, H. J., *Canons and Decrees of the Council of Trent: Original Text with English Translation*, St. Louis: B. Herder Book Co., 1941.

Spicilegium sive Collectio Veterum Aliquot Scriptorum, ed. D. Lucas d'Achery, 2. ed., de la Barre, 3 tom., Parisiis, 1723.

Statuta a Clericis Excalceatis Congregationis SS. Crucis et Passionis D. N. J. C. Servanda, Romae, 1935.

Authors

Aloisius a S. Francisco Paulano, *De Capitulis Habendis in Congregatione Clericorum Excalceatorum SS. Crucis et Passionis D. N. J. C.*, Romae: ex Typographia Pontificia in Instituto Pii X, 1920.

Arregui, Antonius M., *Summarium Theologiae Moralis ad Recentem Codicem Iuris Canonici Accommodatum*, 12. ed., Bilbao: El mensajero del Corazon de Jesus, 1934.

Augustine [Bachofen], Charles, *A Commentary on the New Code of Canon Law*, 8 vols., St. Louis: Herder, Vol. II, 6. ed., 1936; Vol. III, 5. ed., 1938.

Bachofen, Charles A., *Compendium Iuris Regularium*, New York: Benziger, 1903.

Barker, Ernest, *The Dominican Order and Convocation*, Oxford, 1913.

Battandier, Albert, *Guide Canonique pour les Constitutions des Instituts à Voeux Simples*, 3. ed., Paris, 1905.

Berutti, Christophorus, *Institutiones Iuris Canonici*, Vol. III, *De Religiosis*, Romae: Marietti, 1936.

Blat, Albertus, *Commentarium Textus Codicis Iuris Canonici*, 5 vols. in 7, Vol. II, *De Personis*, 2. ed., Romae: Libreria del Collegio Angelico, 1921.

Bouix, D., *Tractatus de Capitulo*, 3. ed., Parisiis, 1882.

Butler, Cuthbert, *Benedictine Monachism,* 2. ed., London: Longmans, Green & Co., 1924.

———, *The Lausiac History of Palladius—Texts and Studies,* VI, 2 vols., Cambridge, 1898-1904.

Calmét, D. Augustin, *Commentaire Littéral, Historique, et Moral sur la Régle de Saint Benôit,* 2 vols. in 1, Paris, 1734.

Cappello, F. M., *Summa Iuris Canonici in Usum Scholarum Concinnata,* 3 vols., Romae: apud Aedes Universitatis Gregorianae, Vols. I-II, 3. ed., 1938-1939.

———, *Summa Iuris Publici Ecclesiastici ad Normam Codicis Iuris Canonici et Recentiorum S. Sedis Documentorum Concinnata,* Romae: Apud Aedes Universitatis Gregorianae, 1923.

Chapman, John, *St. Benedict and the Sixth Century,* London: Sheed & Ward, 1929.

Chelodi, Ioannis, *Ius de Personis iuxta Codicem Iuris Canonici Praemisso Tractatu de Principiis et Fontibus I. C.,* 2 ed., a Ernesto Bertagnolli, Tridenti: Libr. Edit. Tridentinum, 1927.

Chronicon Abbatiae de Evesham, Rolls Series, ed. William Dunn McRay, London, 1863.

Commentarium Pauli Warnefridi Diaconi Casinensis in Regulam S. P. N. Benedicti—Bibliotheca Casinensis, 5 vols., Vol. IV, Casinensi, 1873.

Coronata, Matthaeus Conte a, *Institutiones Iuris Canonici ad Usum Utriusque Cleri et Scholarum,* 5 vols., Vol. I, 2. ed., Taurini: Marietti, 1939.

Creusen, Joseph, *Religious Men and Women in the Code,* 1. English translation by Edward F. Garesché, 3. English ed., revised and edited to conform with the 5. French ed., Milwaukee: Bruce, 1940.

Customary of the Benedictine Monasteries of St. Augustine, Canterbury, and St. Peter, Westminster, 2 vols., Vol. II, ed. by Sir Edward Maunde Thompson, London, 1904.

Delatte, Paul, *The Rule of St. Benedict, a Commentary,* translated by Dom Justin McCann, London: Burns, Oates & Washburn, 1921.

Dictionary, A New English, on Historical Principles, Oxford: Clarendon Press, 1888—

Expositio Regulae ab Hildemaro Tradita, ed. Mittermueller, Regensburg, 1880.

Fanfani, *De Iure Religiosorum ad Normam Codicis Iuris Canonici,* 2. ed., Taurini-Romae: Marietti, 1925.

Feasey, Henry John, *Monasticism, What Is It?,* London, 1898.

Gesta Abbatum Sancti Albani, Rolls Series, 3 vols., ed. Henry Thomas Riley, London, 1867-1869.

Gillet, Pierre, *La Personnalité Juridique en Droit Ecclésiastique, spécialement chez les Décrétistes et les Décrétalistes et dans le Code de Droit Canonique,* Universitas Catholica Lovaniensis, Dissertationes ad gradum magistri in Facultate Theologica consequendum conscriptae, Series II, Tomus 18, Malines: W. Godenne, 1927.

Ioannis Cassiani Conlationes XXIIII, ed. Michael Petsching—*Corpus Scriptorum Ecclesiasticorum Latinorum,* Vol. XIII, Pars II, Vindobonae, 1886.

Knowles, David, *The Monastic Order in England*, Cambridge: University Press, 1940.

Mandonnet, Pierre, *Saint Dominique*, 2 vols., Paris: Desclée, 1938.

Maroto, Phillipus, *Institutiones Iuris Canonici ad Normam Novi Codicis*, 2 vols., Vol. I, Matriti: Editorial del corazon de Maria, 1919.

Martène, Edmond, *De Antiquis Ecclesiae Ritibus*, 4 toms. in 2 vols., Venetiis, 1783.

Memorials of St. Edmund's Abbey, Rolls Series, 3 vols., ed. Thomas Arnold, London, 1890-1896.

Michiels, Gommarus, *Principia Generalia de Personis in Ecclesia*, Belgium: Braaschaat, 1932.

Montalembert, Comte de, *Monks of the West*, with an Introduction by F. A. Gasquet, 6 vols., New York, 1896.

Parsons, Anscar, O.F.M.Cap., *Canonical Elections*, The Catholic University of America Canon Law Studies, n. 118, Washington, D. C.: The Catholic University of America Press, 1939.

Pejška, Josephus, *Ius Canonicum Religiosorum*, 3. ed., Friburgi Brisgoviae: Herder & Co., 1927.

Pellizzarius, Franciscus, *Tractatio de Monialibus*, Venetiis, 1651.

Piatus Montensis, F., *Praelections Iuris Regularis*, 3. ed., 2 vols., Tornaci, 1906.

Schaefer, Timotheus, *De Religiosis ad Normam Codicis Iuris Canonici*, 3. ed., Romae: S. A. L. E. R., 1940.

Schroeder, H. J., *Disciplinary Decrees of the General Councils: Text, Translation, and Commentary*, St. Louis: B. Herder Book Co., 1937.

Van Hove, A., *De Legibus Ecclesiasticis—Commentarium Lovaniense in Codicem Iuris Canonici, editum a Magistris et Doctoribus Universitatis Lovaniensis*, Vol. I, Tom. II, Mechliniae-Romae: H. Dessain, 1930.

Vermeersch, A., *De Religiosis Institutis et Personis Tractatus Canonico-Moralis*, 2. ed., 2 vols., Brugis, 1902-1904.

Vermeersch, A.-Creusen, J., *Epitome Iuris Canonici cum Commentariis ad Scholas et Usum Privatorum*, 3 vols., Vol. I, 6. ed., Romae: H. Dessain, 1937.

Wernz, Franciscus X., *Ius Decretalium*, 6 vols., Vol. III, Romae, 1908.

Wernz, Franciscus X.-Vidal, P., *Ius Canonicum ad Codicis Normam Exactum*, 7 toms. in 8 vols., Romae: apud Aedes Universitatis Gregorianae, Tom. II, *De Personis*, 2. ed., 1928, Tom. III, *De Religiosis*, 1933.

Woywod, Stanislaus, *A Practical Commentary on the Code of Canon Law*, 2 vols., 5. ed., New York: Wagner, 1939.

Zitelli-Natali, Zephyrinus, *Apparatus Iuris Ecclesiastici*, Romae, 1907.

Periodicals

Archiv für Literatur-und Kirchengeschichte des Mittelalters, Berlin-Freiburg im Breisgau, 1885-1890.

Commentarium pro Religiosis (from 1935, *Commentarium pro Religiosis et Missionariis*), Romae, 1920—

Periodica de Re Canonica et Morali utili Praesertim Religiosis et Missionariis, Bruges, 1905.

Quellen und Forschungen zur Geschichte des Dominikanerordens in Deutschland, Leipzig, 1907—

Review for Religious, St. Marys, Kansas, 1942—

Articles

Blat, Albertus, O.P., "De Potestate Superiorum in Religionibus secundum Codicem I.C."—*CpRM*, XVI (1935), 321-353.

Ellis, Adam C., "The General Chapter of Elections in a Religious Congregation" —*RfR*, I (1942), 146-156.

———, "The General Chapter of Affairs in a Religious Congregation"—*RfR*, I (1942), 253-258.

Goyeneche, S., "Consultationes"—*CpR*., III (1922), 222-223; V (1924), 281-282; VII (1926), 390-392; VIII (1927), 31-32.

Larraona, Arcadius, "Commentarium Codicis"—*CpR*, IV (1923), 107-112; VI (1925), 425-431; VII (1926), 30-36, 93-98, 444-448; VIII (1927), 22-30, 102-112.

———, "Consultationes"—*CpR*, II (1921), 340-342.

———, "De Electionibus Religiosorum"—*CpR*, VIII (1927), 177-184, 284-295; IX (1928), 110-114, 329-340; X (1929), 56-57, 265-271.

———, "De Potestate Dominativa Publica in Iure Canonico"—*Acta Congressus Iuridici Internationalis VII Saeculo a Decretalibus Gregorii IX et XIV a Codice Iustiniano Promulgatis, Romae, 12-17 Novembris, 1934*, 5 vols., Romae: apud Custodiam Librariam Pont. Instituti Utriusque Iuris, Vol. IV (1937), 145ss.

Maroto, Phillipus, "Annotationes"—*CpR*, II (1921), 322-329; XV (1934), 346-351.

Scheeben, H. Chr., "Die Konstitutionen des Dominikanerordens unter Jordan von Sachsen"—*Quellen und Forschungen zur Geschichte des Dominikanerordens in Deutschland*, fasc. 38 (1938).

(Vermeersch, A., [?]), "Quaesita Propria Religiosorum, 10"—*Periodica de Re Canonica et Morali*, XI (1923), (153).

ABBREVIATIONS

AAS—*Acta Apostolicae Sedis.*
Bizzarri—*Collectanea in Usum Secretariae Sacrae Congregationis Episcoporum et Regularium.*
Bull. Rom. Taur.—*Bullarium Romanum, ed. Taurinensis.*
CpR—*Commentarium pro Religiosis.*
CpRM—*Commentarium pro Religiosis et Missionariis.*
CSEL—*Corpus Scriptorum Ecclesiasticorum Latinorum.*
Fontes—*Codicis Iuris Canonici Fontes.*
JE—Jaffé-Ewald, *Regesta Pontificum Romanorum. . . .*
JK—Jaffé-Kaltenbrunner, *Regesta Pontificum Romanorum. . . .*
JL—Jaffé-Loewenfeld, *Regesta Pontificum Romanorum. . . .*
MGH—*Monumenta Germaniae Historica.*
MPG—Migne, *Patrologia Graeca.*
MPL—Migne, *Patrologia Latina.*
Normae—*Normae secundum quas Sacra Congregatio Episcoporum et Regularium . . . procedere solet.*
RfR—*Review for Religious.*
S. C. de Religiosis—Sacra Congregatio de Religiosis.
S. C. Ep. et Reg.—Sacra Congregatio Episcoporum et Regularium.
S. C. S. Off.—Sacra Congregatio Sancti Officii.
S. C. super Statu. Reg.—Sacra Congregatio super Statu Regularium.

ALPHABETICAL INDEX

BIOGRAPHICAL NOTE

Gordian Lewis was born on August 14, 1911, in Cincinnati, Ohio. He received his elementary training at Holy Cross parish school of that city. In 1925 he entered the Preparatory Seminary of the Passionist Fathers in Normandy, Mo. He was admitted to the Passionist novitiate in 1929 and made his religious profession on September 23, 1930. He was ordained to the priesthood on June 11, 1938. After one year spent in the study of sermon construction and delivery, he was appointed to teach Canon Law in the Passionist house of studies in Louisville, Ky. In the autumn of 1940 he entered the School of Canon Law of the Catholic University of America, where he received the degree of the Baccalaureate in Canon Law in June, 1941, and the degree of the Licentiate in Canon Law in May, 1942.

CANON LAW STUDIES *

1. FRERIKS, REV. CELESTINE A., C.PP.S., J.C.D., Religious Congregations in Their External Relations, 121 pp., 1916.
2. GALLIHER, REV. DANIEL M., O.P., J.C.D., Canonical Elections, 117 pp., 1917.
3. BORKOWSKI, REV. AURELIUS L., O.F.M., J.C.D., De Confraternitatibus Ecclesiasticis, 136 pp., 1918.
4. CASTILLO, REV. CAYO, J.C.D., Disertacion Historico-Canonica sobre la Potestad del Cabildo en Sede Vacante o Impedida del Vicario Capitular, 99 pp., 1919 (1918).
5. KUBELBECK, REV. WILLIAM J., S.T.B., J.C.D., The Sacred Penitentiaria and Its Relation to Faculties of Ordinaries and Priests, 129 pp., 1918.
6. PETROVITS, REV. JOSEPH, J.C., S.T.D., J.C.D., The New Church Law on Matrimony, X-461 pp., 1919.
7. HICKEY, REV. JOHN J., S.T.B., J.C.D., Irregularities and Simple Impediments in the New Code of Canon Law, 100 pp., 1920.
8. KLEKOTKA, REV. PETER J., S.T.B., J.C.D., Diocesan Consultors, 179 pp., 1920.
9. WANENMACHER, REV. FRANCIS, J.C.D., The Evidence in Ecclesiastical Procedure Affecting the Marriage Bond, 1920 (Printed 1935).
10. GOLDEN, REV. HENRY FRANCIS, J.C.D., Parochial Benefices in the New Code, IV-119 pp., 1921 (Printed 1925).
11. KOUDELKA, REV. CHARLES J., J.C.D., Pastors, Their Rights and Duties According to the New Code of Canon Law, 211 pp., 1921.
12. MELO, REV. ANTONIUS, O.F.M., J.C.D., De Exemptione Regularium, X-188 pp., 1921.
13 SCHAAF, REV. VALENTINE THEODORE, O.F.M., S.T.B., J.C.D., The Cloister, X-180 pp., 1921.
14. BURKE, REV. THOMAS JOSEPH, S.T.D., J.C.D., Competence in Ecclesiastical Tribunals, IV-117 pp., 1922.
15. LEECH, REV. GEORGE LEO, J.C.D., A Comparative Study of the Constitution "Apostolicae Sedis" and the "Codex Juris Canonici," 179 pp., 1922.
16. MOTRY, REV. HUBERT LOUIS, S.T.D., J.C.D., Diocesan Faculties According to the Code of Canon Law, II-167 pp., 1922.
17. MURPHY, REV. GEORGE LAWRENCE, J.C.D., Delinquencies and Penalties in the Administration and the Reception of the Sacraments, IV-121 pp., 1923.
18. O'REILLY, REV. JOHN ANTHONY, S.T.B., J.C.D., Ecclesiastical Sepulture in the New Code of Canon Law, II-129 pp., 1923.

* Below n. 100 only the following numbers are still available: Nn. 3, 4, 9, 25, 34, 57 and 75. Beginning with n. 100 only the following are unavailable: Nn. 100, 101, 102, 104, 105, 107, 108, 109, 111 and 113.

19. MICHALICKA, REV. WENCESLAS CYRILL, O.S.B., J.C.D., Judicial Procedure in Dismissal of Clerical Exempt Religious, 107 pp., 1923.
20. DARGIN, REV. EDWARD VINCENT, S.T.B., J.C.D., Reserved Cases According to the Code of Canon Law, IV-103 pp., 1924.
21. GODFREY, REV. JOHN A., S.T.B., J.C.D., The Right of Patronage According to the Code of Canon Law, 153 pp., 1924.
22. HAGEDORN, REV. FRANCIS EDWARD, J.C.D., General Legislation on Indulgences, II-154 pp., 1924.
23. KING, REV. JAMES IGNATIUS, J.C.D., The Administration of the Sacraments to Dying Non-Catholics, V-141 pp., 1924.
24. WINSLOW, REV. FRANCIS JOSEPH, O.F.M., J.C.D., Vicars and Prefects Apostolic, IV-149 pp., 1924.
25. CORREA, REV. JOSE SERVELION, S.T.L., J.C.D., La Potestad Legislativa de la Iglesia Catolica, IV-127 pp., 1925.
26. DUGAN, REV. HENRY FRANCIS, A.M., J.C.D., The Judiciary Department of the Diocesan Curia, 87 pp., 1925.
27. KELLER, REV. CHARLES FREDERICK, S.T.B., J.C.D., Mass Stipends, 167 pp., 1925.
28. PASCHANG, REV. JOHN LINUS, J.C.D., The Sacramentals According to the Code of Canon Law, 129 pp., 1925.
29. PIONTEK, REV. CYRILLUS, O.F.M., S.T.B., J.C.D., De Indulto Exclaustrationis necnon Saecularizationis, XIII-289 pp., 1925.
30. KEARNEY, REV. RICHARD JOSEPH, S.T.B., J.C.D., Sponsors at Baptism According to the Code of Canon Law, IV-127 pp., 1925.
31. BARTLETT, REV. CHESTER JOSEPH, A.M., LL.B., J.C.D., The Tenure of Parochial Property in the United States of America, V-108 pp., 1926.
32. KILKER, REV. ADRIAN JEROME, J.C.D., Extreme Unction, V-425 pp., 1926.
33. MCCORMICK, REV. ROBERT EMMETT, J.C.D., Confessors of Religious, VIII-266 pp., 1926.
34. MILLER, REV. NEWTON THOMAS, J.C.D., Founded Masses According to the Code of Canon Law, VII-93 pp., 1926.
35. ROELKER, REV. EDWARD G., S.T.D., J.C.D., Principles of Privilege According to the Code of Canon Law, XI-166 pp., 1926.
36. BAKALARCZYK, REV. RICHARDUS, M.I.C., J.U.D., De Novitiatu, VIII-208 pp., 1927.
37. PIZZUTI, REV. LAWRENCE, O.F.M., J.U.L., De Parochis Religiosis, 1927. (Not Printed.)
38. BLILEY, REV. NICHOLAS MARTIN, O.S.B., J.C.D., Altars According to the Code of Canon Law, XIX-132 pp., 1927.
39. BROWN, MR. BRENDAN FRANCIS, A.B., LL.M., J.U.D., The Canonical Juristic Personality with Special Reference to its Status in the United States of America, V-212 pp., 1927.
40. CAVANAUGH, REV. WILLIAM THOMAS, C.P., J.U.D., The Reservation of the Blessed Sacrament, VIII-101 pp., 1927.

41. DOHENY, REV. WILLIAM J., C.S.C., A.B., J.U.D., Church Property: Modes of Acquisition, X-118 pp., 1927.
42. FELDHAUS, REV. ALOYSIUS H., C.PP.S., J.C.D., Oratories, IX-141 pp., 1927.
43. KELLY, REV. JAMES PATRICK, A.B., J.C.D., The Jurisdiction of the Simple Confessor, X-208 pp., 1927.
44. NEUBERGER, REV. NICHOLAS J., J.C.D., Canon 6 or the Relation of the Codex Juris Canonici to the Preceding Legislation, V-95 pp., 1927.
45. O'KEEFE, REV. GERALD MICHAEL, J.C.D., Matrimonial Dispensations, Powers of Bishops, Priests, and Confessors, VIII-232 pp., 1927.
46. QUIGLEY, REV. JOSEPH A. M., A.B., J.C.D., Condemned Societies, 139 pp., 1927.
47. ZAPLOTNIK, REV. JOHANNES LEO, J.C.D., De Vicariis Foraneis, X-142 pp., 1927.
48. DUSKIE, REV. JOHN ALOYSIUS, A.B., J.C.D., The Canonical Status of the Orientals in the United States, VIII-196 pp., 1928.
49. HYLAND, REV. FRANCIS EDWARD, J.C.D., Excommunication, Its Nature, Historical Development and Effects, VIII-181 pp., 1928.
50. REINMANN, REV. GERALD JOSEPH, O.M.C., J.C.D., The Third Order Secular of Saint Francis, 201 pp., 1928.
51. SCHENK, REV. FRANCIS J., J.C.D., The Matrimonial Impediments of Mixed Religion and Disparity of Cult, XVI-318 pp., 1929.
52. COADY, REV. JOHN JOSEPH, S.T.D., J.U.D., A.M., The Appointment of Pastors, VIII-150 pp., 1929.
53. KAY, REV. THOMAS HENRY, J.C.D., Competence in Matrimonial Procedure, VIII-164 pp., 1929.
54. TURNER, REV. SIDNEY JOSEPH, C.P., J.U.D., The Vow of Poverty, XLIX-217 pp., 1929.
55. KEARNEY, REV. RAYMOND A., A.B., S.T.D., J.C.D., The Principles of Delegation, VII-149 pp., 1929.
56. CONRAN, REV. EDWARD JAMES, A.B., J.C.D., The Interdict,, V-163 pp., 1930.
57. O'NEILL, REV. WILLIAM H., J.C.D., Papal Rescripts of Favor, VII-218 pp., 1930.
58. BASTNAGEL, REV. CLEMENT VINCENT, J.U.D., The Appointment of Parochial Adjutants and Assistants, XV-257 pp., 1930.
59. FERRY, REV. WILLIAM A., A.B., J.C.D., Stole Fees, V-136 pp., 1930.
60. COSTELLO, REV. JOHN MICHAEL, A.B., J.C.D., Domicile and Quasi-Domicile, VII-201 pp., 1930.
61. KREMER, REV. MICHAEL NICHOLAS, A.B., S.T.B., J.C.D., Church Support in the United States, VI-136 pp., 1930.
62. ANGULO, REV. LUIS, C.M., J.C.D., Legislation de la Iglesia sobre la intencion en la application de la Santa Misa, VII-104 pp., 1931.
63. FREY, REV. WOLFGANG NORBERT, O.S.B., A.B., J.C.D., The Act of Religious Profession, VIII-174 pp., 1931.

64. ROBERTS, REV. JAMES BRENDAN, A.B., J.C.D., The Banns of Marriage, XIV-140 pp., 1931.
65. RYDER, REV. RAYMOND ALOYSIUS, A.B., J.C.D., Simony, IX-151 pp., 1931.
66. CAMPAGNA, REV. ANGELO, PH.D., J.U.D., Il Vicario Generale del Vescovo, VII-205 pp., 1931.
67. COX, REV. JOSEPH GODFREY, A.B., J.C.D., The Administration of Seminaries, VI-124 pp., 1931.
68. GREGORY, REV. DONALD J., J.U.D., The Pauline Privilege, XV-165 pp., 1931.
69. DONOHUE, REV. JOHN F., J.C.D., The Impediment of Crime, VII-110 pp., 1931.
70. DOOLEY, REV. EUGENE A., O.M.I., J.C.D., Church Law on Sacred Relics, IX-143 pp., 1931.
71. ORTH, REV. CLEMENT RAYMOND, O.M.C., J.C.D., The Approbation of Religious Institutes, 171 pp., 1931.
72. PERNICONE, REV. JOSEPH M., A.B., J.C.D., The Ecclesiastical Prohibition of Books, XII-267 pp., 1932.
73. CLINTON, REV. CONNELL, A.B., J.C.D., The Paschal Precept, IX-108 pp., 1932.
74. DONNELLY, REV. FRANCIS B., A.M., S.T.L., J.C.D., The Diocesan Synod, VIII-125 pp., 1932.
75. TORRENTE, REV. CAMILO, C.M.F., J.C.D., Las Processiones Sagradas, V-145 pp., 1932.
76. MURPHY, REV. EDWIN J., C.PP.S., J.C.D., Suspension Ex Informata Conscientia, XI-122 pp., 1932.
77. MACKENZIE, REV. ERIC F., A.M., S.T.L., J.C.D., The Delict of Heresy in its Commission, Penalization, Absolution, VII-124 pp., 1932.
78. LYONS, REV. AVITUS E., S.T.B., J.C.D., The Collegiate Tribunal of First Instance, XI-147 pp., 1932.
79. CONNOLLY, REV. THOMAS A., J.C.D., Appeals, XI-195 pp., 1932.
80. SANGMEISTER, REV. JOSEPH V., A.B., J.C.D., Force and Fear as Precluding Matrimonial Consent, V-211 pp., 1932.
81. JAEGER, REV. LEO A., A.B., J.C.D., The Administration of Vacant and Quasi-Vacant Episcopal Sees in the United States, IX-229 pp., 1932.
82. RIMLINGER, REV. HERBERT T., J.C.D., Error Invalidating Matrimonial Consent, VII-79 pp., 1932.
83. BARRETT, REV. JOHN D. M., S.S., J.C.D., A Comparative Study of the Third Plenary Council of Baltimore and the Code, IX-221 pp., 1932.
84. CARBERRY, REV. JOHN J., PH.D., S.T.D., J.C.D., The Juridical Form of Marriage, X-177 pp., 1934.
85. DOLAN, REV. JOHN L., A.B., J.C.D., The Defensor Vinculi, XII-157 pp., 1934.
86. HANNAN, REV. JEROME D., A.M., S.T.D., LL.B., J.C.D., The Canon Law of Wills, IX-517 pp., 1934.

87. LEMIEUX, REV. DELISE A., A.M., J.C.D., The Sentence in Ecclesiastical Procedure, IX-131 pp., 1934.
88. O'ROURKE, REV. JAMES J., A.B., J.C.D., Parish Registers, VII-109 pp., 1934.
89. TIMLIN, REV. BARTHOLOMEW, O.F.M., A.M., J.C.D., Conditional Matrimonial Consent, X-381 pp., 1934.
90. WAHL, REV. FRANCIS X., A.B., J.C.D., The Matrimonial Impediments of Consanguinity and Affinity, VI-125 pp., 1934.
91. WHITE, REV. ROBERT J., A.B., LL.B., S.T.B., J.C.D., Canonical Ante-Nuptial Promises and the Civil Law, VI-152 pp., 1934.
92. HERRERA, REV. ANTONIO PARRA, O.C.D., J.C.D., Legislacion Ecclesiastica sobra el Ayuno y la Abstinencia, XI-191 pp., 1935.
93. KENNEDY, REV. EDWIN J., J.C.D., The Special Matrimonial Process in Cases of Evident Nullity, X-165 pp., 1935.
94. MANNING, REV. JOHN J., A.B., J.C.D., Presumption of Law in Matrimonial Procedure, XI-111 pp., 1935.
95. MOEDER, REV. JOHN M., J.C.D., The Proper Bishop for Ordination and Dimissorial Letters, VII-135 pp., 1935.
96. O'MARA, REV. WILLIAM A., A.B., J.C.D., Canonical Causes for Matrimonial Dispensations, IX-155 pp., 1935.
97. REILLY, REV. PETER, J.C.D., Residence of Pastors, IX-81 pp., 1935.
98. SMITH, REV. MARINER T., O.P., S.T.Lr., J.C.D., The Penal Law for Religious, VIII-169 pp., 1935.
99. WHALEN, REV. DONALD W., A.M., J.C.D., The Value of Testimonial Evidence in Matrimonial Procedure, XIII-297 pp., 1935.
100. CLEARY, REV. JOSEPH F., J.C.D., Canonical Limitations on the Alienation of Church Property, VIII-141 pp., 1936.
101. GLYNN, REV. JOHN C., J.C.D., The Promoter of Justice, XX-337 pp., 1936.
102. BRENNAN, REV. JAMES H., S.S., M.A., S.T.B., J.C.D., The Simple Convalidation of Marriage, VI-135 pp., 1937.
103. BRUNINI, REV. JOSEPH BERNARD, J.C.D., The Clerical Obligations of Canons 139 and 142, X-121 pp., 137.
104. CONNOR, REV. MAURICE, A.B., J.C.D., The Administrative Removal of Pastors, VIII-159 pp., 1937.
105. GUILFOYLE, REV. MERLIN JOSEPH, J.C.D., Custom, XI-144 pp., 1937.
106. HUGHES, REV. JAMES AUSTIN, A.B., A.M., J.C.D., Witnesses in Criminal Trials of Clerics, IX-140 pp., 1937.
107. JANSEN, REV. RAYMOND J., A.B., S.T.L., J.C.D., Canonical Provisions for Catechetical Instruction, VII-153 pp., 1937.
108. KEALY, REV. JOHN JAMES, A.B., J.C.D., The Introductory Libellus in Church Court Procedure, XI-121 pp., 1937.
109. MCMANUS, REV. JAMES EDWARD, C.SS.R., J.C.D., The Administration of Temporal Goods in Religious Institutes, XVI-196 pp., 1937.

110. MORIARTY, REV. EUGENE JAMES, J.C.D., Oaths in Ecclesiastical Courts, X-115 pp., 1937.

111. RAINIER, REV. ELIGIUS GEORGE, C.SS.R., J.C.D., Suspension of Clerics, XVII-249 pp., 1937.

112. REILLY, REV. THOMAS F., C.SS.R., J.C.D., Visitation of Religious, VI-195 pp., 1938.

113. MORIARTY, REV. FRANCIS E., C.SS.R., J.C.D., The Extraordinary Absolution from Censures, XV-334 pp., 1938.

114. CONNOLLY, REV. NICHOLAS P., J.C.D., The Canonical Erection of Parishes, X-132 pp., 1938.

115. DONOVAN, REV. JAMES JOSEPH, J.C.D., The Pastor's Obligation in Prenuptial Investigation, XII-322 pp., 1938.

116. HARRIGAN, REV. ROBERT J., M.A., S.T.B., J.C.D., The Radical Sanation of Invalid Marriages, VIII-208 pp., 1938.

117. BOFFA, REV. CONRAD HUMBERT, J.C.D., Canonical Provisions for Catholic Schools, VII-211 pp., 1939.

118. PARSONS, REV. ANSCAR JOHN, O.M.Cap., J.C.D., Canonical Elections, XII-236 pp., 1939.

119. REILLY, REV. EDWARD MICHAEL, A.B., J.C.D., The General Norms of Dispensation, XII-156 pp., 1939.

120. RYAN, REV. GERALD ALOYSIUS, A.B., J.C.D., Principles of Episcopal Jurisdiction, XII-172 pp., 1939.

121. BURTON, REV. FRANCIS JAMES, C.S.C., A.B., J.C.D., A Commentary on Canon 1125, X-222 pp., 1940.

122. MIASKIEWICZ, REV. FRANCIS SIGISMUND, J.C.D., Supplied Jurisdiction According to Canon 209, XII-340 pp., 1940.

123. RICE, REV. PATRICK WILLIAM, A.B., J.C.D., Proof of Death in Prenuptial Investigation, VIII-156 pp., 1940.

124. ANGLIN, REV. THOMAS FRANCIS, M.S., J.C.D., The Eucharistic Fast, VIII-183 pp., 1941.

125. COLEMAN, REV. JOHN JEROME, J.C.D., The Minister of Confirmation, VI-153 pp., 1941.

126. DOWNS, REV. JOSEPH EMMANUEL, A.B., J.C.D., The Concept of Clerical Immunity, XI-163 pp., 1941.

127. ESSWEIN, REV. ANTHONY ALBERT, J.C.D., Extrajudicial Penal Powers of Ecclesiastical Superiors, X-144 pp., 1941.

128. FARRELL, REV. BENJAMIN FRANCIS, M.A., S.T.L., J.C.D., The Rights and Duties of the Local Ordinary Regarding Congregations of Women Religious of Pontifical Approval, V-195 pp., 1941.

129. FEENEY, REV. THOMAS JOHN, A.B., S.T.L., J.C.D., Restitutio in Integrum, VI-169 pp., 1941.

130. FINDLAY, REV. STEPHEN WILLIAM, O.S.B., A.B., J.C.D., Canonical Norms Governing the Deposition and Degradation of Clerics, XVII-279 pp., 1941.

131. Goodwine, Rev. John, A.B., S.T.L., J.C.D., The Right of the Church to Acquire Property, VIII-119 pp., 1941.
132. Heston, Rev. Edward Louis, C.S.C., Ph.D., S.T.D., J.C.D., The Alienation of Church Property in the United States, XII-222 pp., 1941.
133. Hogan, Rev. James John, A.B., S.T.L., J.C.D., Judicial Advocates and Procurators, XIII-200 pp., 1941.
134. Kealy, Rev. Thomas M., A.B., Litt.B., J.C.D., Dowry of Women Religious, IX-152 pp., 1941.
135. Keene, Rev. Michael James, O.S.B., J.C.D., Religious Ordinaries and Canon 198, V-164 pp., 1942.
136. Kerin, Rev. Charles A., S.S., M.A., S.T.B., J.C.D., The Privation of Christian Burial, XVI-279 pp., 1941.
137. Louis, Rev. William Francis, M.A., J.C.D., Diocesan Archives, X-101 pp., 1941.
138. McDevitt, Rev. Gilbert Joseph, A.B., J.C.D., Legitimacy and Legitimation, X-247 pp., 1941.
139. McDonough, Rev. Thomas Joseph, A.B., J.C.D., Apostolic Administrators, X-217 pp., 1941.
140. Meier, Rev. Carl Anthony, A.B., J.C.D., Penal Administrative Procedure Against Negligent Pastors, XI-240 pp., 1941.
141. Schmidt, Rev. John Rogg, A.B., J.C.D., The Principles of Authentic Interpretation in Canon 17 of the Code of Canon Law, XII-331 pp., 1941.
142. Slafkosky, Rev. Andrew Leonard, A.B., J.C.D., The Canonical Episcopal Visitation of the Diocese, X-197 pp., 1941.
143. Swoboda, Rev. Innocent Robert, O.F.M., J.C.D., Ignorance in Relation to the Imputability of Delicts, IX-271 pp., 1941.
144. Dubé, Rev. Arthur Joseph, A.B., J.C.D., The General Principles for the Reckoning of Time in Canon Law, VIII-299 pp., 1941.
145. McBride, Rev. James T., A.B., J.C.D., Incardination and Excardination of Seculars, XX-585 pp., 1941.
146. Król, Rev. John T., J.C.D., The Defendant in Ecclesiastical Trials, XII-207 pp., 1942.
147. Comyns, Rev. Joseph J., C.SS.R., A.B., J.C.D., Papal and Episcopal Administration of Church Property, XIV-155 pp., 1942.
148. Barry, Rev. Garrett Francis, O.M.I., J.C.D., Violation of the Cloister, XII-260 pp., 1942.
149. Bolduc, Rev. Gatien, C.S.V., A.B., S.T.L., J.C.D., Les Études dans les Religions Cléricales, VIII-155 pp., 1942.
150. Boyle, Rev. David John, M.A., J.C.D., The Juridic Effects of Moral Certitude on Pre-Nuptial Guarantees, XII-188 pp., 1942.
151. Canavan, Rev. Walter Joseph, M.A., Litt.D., J.C.D., The Profession of Faith, XII-143 pp., 1942.
152. Desrochers, Rev. Bruno, A.B., Ph.L., S.T.B., J.C.D., Le Premier Concile Plénier de Québec et le Code de Droit Canonique, XIV-186 pp., 1942.

153. Dillon, Rev. Robert Edward, A.B., J.C.D., Common Law Marriage, X-148 pp., 1942.
154. Dodwell, Rev. Edward John, Ph.D., S.T.B., J.C.L., The Time and Place for the Celebration of Marriage.
155. Donnellan, Rev. Thomas Andrew, A.B., J.C.D., The Obligation of the Missa pro Populo, VII-131 pp., 1942.
156. Eltz, Rev. Louis Anthony, A.B., J.C.L., Cooperation in Crime.
157. Gass, Rev. Sylvester Francis, M.A., J.C.D., Ecclesiastical Pensions, XI-206 pp., 1942.
158. Guiniven, Rev. John Joseph, C.SS.R., J.C.D., The Precept of Hearing Mass, XIV-188 pp., 1942.
159. Gulczynski, Rev. John Theophilus, J.C.D., The Desecration and Violation of Churches.
160. Hammill, Rev. John Leo, M.A., J.C.D., The Obligations of the Traveler According to Canon 14, VIII-204 pp., 1942.
161. Haydt, Rev. John Joseph, A.B., J.C.D., Reserved Benefices, XI-148 pp., 1942.
162. Huser, Rev. Roger John, O.F.M., A.B., J.C.D., The Crime of Abortion in Canon Law.
163. Kearney, Rev. Francis Patrick, A.B., S.T.L., J.C.L., The Principles of Canon 1127.
164. Linahen, Rev. Leo James, S.T.L., J.C.D., De Absolutione Complicis In Peccato Turpi, 114 pp., 1942.
165. McCloskey, Rev. Joseph Aloysius, A.B., J.C.D., The Subject of Ecclesiastical Law According to Canon 12, XVII-246 pp., 1942.
166. O'Neill, Rev. Francis Joseph, C.SS.R., J.C.D., The Dismissal of Religious in Temporary Vows, XIII-220 pp., 1942.
167. Prince, Rev. John Edward, A.B., S.T.B., J.C.D., The Diocesan Chancellor, X-136 pp., 1942.
168. Riesner, Rev. Albert Joseph, C.SS.R., J.C.D., Apostates and Fugitives from Religious Institutes, IX-168 pp., 1942.
169. Stenger, Rev. Joseph Bernard, J.C.D., The Mortgaging of Church Property, 186 pp., 1942.
170. Waldron, Rev. Joseph Francis, A.B., J.C.D., The Minister of Baptism, XII-197 pp., 1942.
171. Willett, Rev. Robert Albert, J.C.D., The Probative Value of Documents in Ecclesiastical Trials, X-124 pp., 1942.
172. Woeber, Rev. Edward Martin, M.A., J.C.D., The Interpellations, XII-161 pp., 1942.
173. Benko, Rev. Matthew Aloysius, O.S.B.. M.A., J.C.L., The Abbot *Nullius*.
174. Christ, Rev. Joseph James, M.A., S.T.L., J.C.L., Dispensation from Vindicative Penalties.
175. Clancy, Rev. Patrick M. J., O.P., A.B., S.T.Lr., J.C.L., The Local Religious Superior.

176. CLARKE, REV. THOMAS JAMES, J.C.L., Parish Societies.
177. CONNOLLY, REV. JOHN PATRICK, S.T.L., J.C.L., Synodal Examiners and Parish Priest Consultors.
178. DRUMM, REV. WILLIAM MARTIN, A.B., J.C.L., Hospital Chaplains.
179. FLANAGAN, REV. BERNARD JOSEPH, A.B., S.T.L., J.C.L., The Canonical Erection of Religious Houses.
180. KELLEHER, REV. STEPHEN JOSEPH, A.B., S.T.B., J.C.L., Discussions with Non-Catholics: Canonical Legislation.
181. LEWIS, REV. GORDIAN, C.P., J.C.L., Chapters in Religious Institutes.
182. MARX, REV. ADOLPH, J.C.L., The Declaration of Nullity of Marriages Contracted Outside the Church.
183. MATULENAS, REV. RAYMOND ANTHONY, O.S.B., A.B., J.C.L., Communication, a Source of Privileges.
184. O'LEARY, REV. CHARLES GERARD, C.SS.R., Religious Dismissed After Perpetual Profession.
185. POWER, REV. CORNELIUS MICHAEL, J.C.L., The Blessing of Cemeteries.
186. SHUHLER, REV. RALPH VINCENT, O.S.A., J.C.L., Privileges of Religious to Absolve and Dispense.
187. ZIOLKOWSKI, REV. THADDEUS STANISLAUS, A.B., J.C.L., The Consecration and Blessing of Churches.

www.ingramcontent.com/pod-product-compliance
Lightning Source LLC
LaVergne TN
LVHW050231080826
844660LV00012B/510

* 9 7 8 0 8 1 3 2 2 3 7 0 4 *